DO

1. What person
   responded to
   man?"

2. What hit film inspired the use of two separate scripts and two separate films in the shooting of SUPERMAN?

3. What modern miracle of our century was used for the first time as a publicity mechanism for SUPERMAN?

4. How many candidates were considered for the Superman role?

5. How many "opticals" were used in the movie?

6. What was Marlon Brando's salary for 13 days' work?

7. What best-selling novelist wrote the original screenplay?

8. What terrifying accident was interpreted by the makers of SUPERMAN as an omen that the film was bound to be a "smash?"

9. What part of Gene Hackman's costuming added $52,000 a day to the filming costs?

10. Why the SUPERMAN lot was closed to reporters and all activities declared TOP SECRET?

**Discover the answers to these
and hundreds of your own questions in**

THE MAKING OF SUPERMAN
THE MOVIE

The Making of Superman
the movie

BY
DAVID MICHAEL PETROU

UNIVERSAL

A UNIVERSAL BOOK

published by
the Paperback Division of
W. H. ALLEN & Co. Ltd.

A Universal Book
Published in 1978
by the Paperback Division of
W. H. Allen & Co. Ltd
A Howard and Wyndham Company
44 Hill Street, London W1X 8LB

First published in the United States of America
by Warner Books, 1978
Printed in Great Britain by
Richard Clay (The Chaucer Press) Ltd, Bungay, Suffolk

To the indefatigable Anita Loos, for whom
the superlative *super* is truly fitting . . .

Foreword

There is a certain pleasant irony in the fact that the story behind the making of "Superman" should be written by someone who doesn't quite clear five feet, three inches in height. But then, our Executive Producer, Ilya Salkind, is barely a few inches taller, and his father, the matchless Alexander Salkind, without whom the entire multi-million-dollar project would never have made it off the ground, could see eye-to-eye with one of L. Frank Baum's Munchkins. All of which goes to prove that someone (I think it must have been Napoleon) once said: "You don't have to be big to have brains." For though we short people are often "topped," rarely are we bested. Chris Reeve—eat your heart out!

In addition to thanking the producers, director Dick Donner, assistant to the producers Maria Monreal, and the entire cast and crew, I want to express my gratitude to the staff of Warner Books, and to DC Comics president Sol Harrison and everyone at Warner Brothers, for all their assistance, cooperation and advice. Naturally, I acknowledge a special debt to the two brilliant creators of Superman, Jerry Siegel and Joe Shuster.

To all the talented men and women who worked on this film and made it something unique among motion pictures, my deep appreciation.

Summer, 1978

David Michael Petrou
Pinewood Studios

Introduction

SUPERMAN, THE LEGEND

*"I teach you the Superman.
Man is something that is to be surpassed."*

—Friedrich Nietzsche, *Thus Spake Zarathustra*

"Look! Up in the sky. It's a bird! It's a plane. . . ."

For millions of Americans and tens of millions of people throughout the world, those familiar words have one unmistakable meaning. They herald the arrival of the twentieth century's most dynamic champion . . . SUPERMAN!

Born in the Depression era, Superman exerted an instant, universal appeal which has spanned the decades undiminished. In an age painfully short of heroes and desperately in need of them, Superman continues to lay unchallenged claim to the triple crown as the world's most enduring, most profitable and most popular fictional superstar.

The legend of Superman is a fantastic phenomenon around the globe, where the ongoing saga is today published in eight separate comic magazines, available in more than thirty-eight nations and printed in fifteen different languages.

And one has only to visit a major store or shopping

center in any of these countries to see the results of this sustained *"Supermania"*—in books, toys, T-shirts, watches, rings, records, decals, posters, paper products and party goods, socks, shoes, sweaters, sheets and towels. And the celebrated red-and-yellow Superman "S" can be seen emblazoned everywhere, even in the most unlikely places: from the backs of leather jackets to the backsides of jeans; from the rear door of a rock star's Rolls-Royce to the woven wicker of a rickshaw in Hong Kong; on surfboards, schoolbooks, airplanes and subway cars— even on men's briefs! The jokes, spoofs, take-offs and satires are almost endless. Most of us are familiar with the Superman references which have adorned recent magazine covers: cartoons of Super "Henry the K" (Kissinger) rocketing around the globe, Barbra Streisand clad only in a white T-shirt emblazoned with the famous logo, even U.S. Energy Secretary James Schlesinger decked out in crimson cloak and tights (where was *he* when the lights went out in New York?). And like *Peanuts*, Superman has even been found to have theological and spiritual implications—a delicate area in which *this* author does not intend to intrude. (Though, it should be noted, the "Superman" story and the screenplay draw heavily on familiar religious elements, most obviously the discovery of the baby Kal-El, much like that of Moses, and the almost mystical bond between him and his father, Jor-El.)

The actual genesis of Superman took place in surroundings somewhat less exotic than Krypton: Cleveland, Ohio, in 1933 . . . in the most painful phase of the Great Depression, the days of breadlines and Bonus Marchers and "Brother, Can You Spare a Dime?" It was a time when the world's morale was pitifully low and in need of something more than Arabian sheiks and knights in shining armor flashing across the silver screen, or posturing politicians promising that prosperity was just around the corner.

As it happened, a high-school student in Ohio did have an answer for that need. Jerry Siegel was a teen-ager of considerable creative powers, possessed of a fantastic imagination and a seemingly insatiable appetite for excitement, action and adventure. Oppressed by the grim reality everywhere around him, Siegel escaped into a world of fiction and fantasy, consuming a steady diet of short stories, science fiction, Saturday matinees—and, of course, the action serials in the multitude of pulp magazines that blossomed on the newsstands. As a re-porter for the *Glenville Torch*, his high-school news-paper, young Siegel reviewed and recommended the very best of what he had seen and read, conveying his own enthusiasm to his peers. One of Siegel's favorites was the hard-hitting *Doc Savage* series, created by Lester Dent, under the pen name of Kenneth Robeson. Savage, officially known as "the Man of Bronze," was an amaz-ingly dynamic hero, recognized for his almost super-human abilities—and was indeed often referred to as "a superman." In 1932 Philip Wylie's novel *Gladiator* appeared, featuring a central character who was yet another superhuman, but with attributes more spectacu-lar and sharply defined than Savage's. He could bound "forty feet into the air," deflect a hail of bullets, and race "at an abnormal pace." The idea of a man pos-sessed of strengths and talents beyond those of other men obviously made a considerable impression on young Siegel, voraciously reading every tale of adventure he could get his hands on—articles, short stories, novels— perhaps delving into Greek mythology (after all, he named the planet of his hero's origin Krypton, from the Greek word *kryptos*, referring to a hidden or secret place) with its tales of the superhuman Prometheus and Hercules, or works as recent as Nietzsche's philosophy, which first popularized the term "Superman."

Superman . . . superhuman . . . fantastic strength . . . incredible abilities. . . . Slowly, inexorably, this imagined amalgam of action and adventure, of fantasy and science fiction, began to coalesce in young Siegel's mind to come together as a single idea: a recognizable form, yet something altogether new and distinctly different. Something beyond what had already been done.

And, tossing in bed on a sultry summer evening, as Siegel recalled much later, "All of a sudden it hits me. I conceive a character like Samson, Hercules and all the strong men I ever heard of rolled into one. Only more so."

Only more so. That seemed to be the key: going a step further than anyone else had gone. Siegel's excitement was impossible to contain; early the next morning, he dashed over to the home of his friend, Joe Shuster, an enthusiastic and talented amateur illustrator. Shuster was immediately fired by Siegel's intense creative enthusiasm. Quickly, he endowed Siegel's idea with visual substance. In these initial sketches, some still familiar trademarks are clearly evident—the bold block letters curving ever so slightly, a muscular, athletic figure with a square-set jaw and jet black hair sporting a forelock. Soon the boys were deeply engrossed in plotting their first adventure. Superman had been born.

Like most initiators, Siegel and Shuster sadly discovered the difficulty of passing along their enthusiasm. The first Superman story, "Reign of the Superman," appeared in Siegel's amateur magazine, *Science Fiction*, in January, 1933. But it was six years before their creation achieved commercial publication, in spite of their many attempts to market it. In 1935, after completing high school, the two boys launched their professional careers at what is now DC Comics, Inc. And so electrically successful was their work—Shuster's bold expressive art and Siegel's fast-paced, imaginative copy—that the publishers prospered sufficiently to take a chance in 1937 on a comic magazine completely composed of original material. That was *Detective Comics*, featuring an entirely new character named Slam Bradley, created by Shuster and Siegel. After that venture succeeded, the publishers were finally prepared to gamble on the boys' long-ignored personal favorite. So in June, 1938, Superman burst forth on the cover of Vol. 1, No. 1 of *Action Comics*. Cost, one dime. A copy in mint condition today goes for $5,000.

With this publication, an American legend was born. For, in fact, Superman is the first comic-hero superstar. He revolutionized an industry. It may not be too much to say that he *created* one.

"Only three fictional heroes of the past century have so gripped the English-speaking world," wrote Richard A. Lupoff in *Edgar Rice Burroughs: Master of Adventure*. "Conan Doyle's Sherlock Holmes, Siegel and Shuster's Superman and Burroughs' Tarzan."

The principal attraction of Superman is the combination of his uniqueness with his very recognizable humanity. He is from another planet, another world. His powers are awesome. His strength is unparalleled. He is, in effect, immortal. Yet the baby Kal-El arrives on Earth an orphan. He is brought up with ordinary, everyday values, by ordinary, everyday people (the Kents), in an ordinary, everyday place (Smallville). Consequently, he is imbued with a strong feeling of love and a sense of responsibility for the world at large. And when he chooses to conceal his true identity, he "invents" Clark Kent by drawing on his own childhood experience. Clark is bumbling, shy, unsure of himself. But he is also gentle, courteous, honest; above all, to readers everywhere, he is vulnerable and identifiably human. And in contrast to other popular fictional heroes possessing double identities—Don Diego/Zorro or Bruce Wayne/Batman—*Clark Kent is the counterfeit* and Superman, all-righteous, all-just, all-powerful, is the reality.

The popularity of the new hero was so immediate and widespread that soon the "Superman" sequences in *Action Comics* were enlarged and expanded. And Mort Weisinger, one of the first of the major "Superman"

—13—

editors, broadened the story possibilities by creating out-landish adventures for the pivotal "Superman" char-acters. Naturally, Superman found himself on an increas-ing number of *Action Comics* covers, and eventually the parent company launched a completely separate "Super-man" imprint.

As the legend grew and spread across America and beyond, "Superman" made the first of many leaps from the printed to the spoken word.

The "Superman" radio program premiered on Feb-ruary 12, 1940, as a three-times-weekly broadcast. It soon became one of the most popular programs on the Mutual Network. Clayton ("Bud") Collyer, who would become well-known as a major television personality, was the inspiring voice of the Man of Steel, with Joan Alexander as reporter Lois Lane and Julian Noa as the crusty but benign Perry White.

In the next year, "Superman" made the transition to several media, starting in 1941 with Max Fleischer's celebrated cartoons. In 1942, a novel entitled *Superman* was written by George Lowther and achieved notable success. Still later came the highly popular "Superman" serials produced by Columbia Studios. Two 15-episode motion pictures were made, "Superman" in 1948 and "Atom Man vs. Superman" in 1950, both starring Kirk Alyn as Superman and Noel Neill as Lois Lane. Each episode pitted the Man of Steel against seemingly insur-mountable odds, and, in the tradition followed from Pearl White on, they ended with a maddening "to be continued" just at the point of climax, thus ensuring for next week a packed theater of enthusiastic fans cling-ing to the edges of their seats.

The success of these serials led the studio to make a feature film entitled "Superman and the Mole Men" (featuring George Reeves as Superman and Phyllis Coates as Lois Lane) which largely followed the serials in style. And soon after, the new national novelty, television, became a forum for Shuster and Siegel's superlative hero.

With television, Superman came into the living rooms of millions of Americans, increasing the popularity of the character and broadening the horizon of the Superman myth. Millions of children tied blankets around their necks and swooped through their homes, emulating their idol.

The "Adventures of Superman" went into production at RKO-Pathé Studios in California in 1951 and continued at various other studios until 1957. Originally starring Reeves and Coates, the series continued in 1953 with Reeves and the original screen Lois, Noel Neill, Jack Larson as Jimmy Olsen, John Hamilton as Perry White and Robert Shayne as Inspector Henderson. It was this cast that Americans came to know as the "Superman" family.

In the years since the television show ceased production, the renown of Superman has increased rather than diminished. The TV series is one of the most popular reruns on the air. While the series was still filming, 20th Century-Fox released a string of five "Superman" "features" compiled from fifteen of the most successful episodes of the TV broadcast. In 1958, a pilot film for a "Superpup" television show met with little success, due largely to scripting and production problems. "The Adventures of Superboy," an ill-conceived successor to the George Reeves series, appeared in April, 1961, and did little more than generate hope that a worthy contemporary vehicle for the Superman legend would be found.

More successful was the 1966 Robert Benton—David and Leslie Newman musical on Broadway, "It's a Bird . . . It's a Plane . . . It's Superman!" And in 1973, Warner Brothers offered for non-theatrical screenings a compilation of four color episodes of the "Adventures of Superman," vintage examples of the very best of the series.

After World War II, during which he dealt super havoc to Axis foes, the comic-book Superman could "relax" a bit, battling more comical combatants like Mr. Mxyzptlk, Toyman and the Prankster instead of the Nazis.

The appearance of Superboy (the young Superman) and new and diverse characters like Supergirl, Krypto the Superdog—and something as outrageous as Superhorse—broadened Superman's horizons and increased tenfold the possibilities for potential adventure as Superman changed with the times.

It is fascinating to observe how Superman matured and developed over the years. In the earliest adventures he could leap over tall buildings and bound an eighth of a mile. Still later he was literally flying. His powers increased, his special "senses" emerged—x-ray vision, super hearing, super breath—and his invincibility became more firmly established. Early on, nothing short of "a bursting shell could penetrate his skin." Now even a hydrogen bomb poses no particular threat.

Naturally, as his strength increased, so did the potential deadliness of kryptonite. As it was initially conceived, kryptonite was merely the transformed radioactive remnant of Superman's home planet, which could enfeeble only a native of Krypton. But soon it emerged as fatal—the *one* thing that could *kill* Superman.

As Superman changed, so did his family, friends and foes. Jor-L, his father, and Lora, his mother, became Jor-El and Lara. John and Mary Kent, his Smallville foster parents, became Eben and Sarah in the Lowther novel (Clark, Sarah's maiden name, provided Superman with his first name). Currently they are known as Jonathan and Martha Kent.

Even Lex Luthor—the evil genius who is the Man of Steel's arch-antagonist—was initially introduced with thick, straight red locks. Today he is portrayed as bald.

While Superman once acted independently of many legal formalities, he is now more punctilious. In recent comic issues he has even gone through the correct diplomatic channels to obtain "air rights" from the United Nations in order to breach "foreign" air space!

The *Daily Planet* has long since been sold to Galaxy Communications and Morgan Edge has supplanted Perry White as the *Planet*'s managing editor.

The comic-book Clark Kent is now a savvy and stylish television newscaster with natty European-cut clothing in the best tradition of hip investigative reporters. His relationships with other people, particularly Lois Lane, are more complex. Perhaps mindful of the Women's Movement, Clark regards Lois as an equal, if not a superior, in their professional and personal relationships. And the natural ambivalence between Clark Kent and Superman has become much more conspicuous. Without question, Superman is in step with the seventies.

But while that which is variable about Superman has been modernized, the myth remains as solid and secure as it was forty years ago. And many of the attempted alterations in the legend backfired spectacularly—most memorably when "Superman's" recent comic-magazine editors tried unsuccessfully to do away with kryptonite. Perhaps Morgan Edge had the final word on Superman's one vulnerability when he said in a classic sequence: "I don't trust *anyone* who can't be stopped! A wise man once said, 'Power corrupts. And absolute power corrupts absolutely'!"

In this film, the first major motion picture of "Superman," that legend has been carefully preserved, renewed, expanded and revitalized. If its makers' dreams are realized, it will convey to even larger audiences the fun, the adventure, the fantasy and the basic spirit of "truth and justice" that Shuster and Siegel envisioned back in 1933—and in a more imaginatively spectacular way than even those two young boys from Ohio ever could have dreamed.

Ilya Salkind, the executive producer, has captured the

essence of that spirit quite simply: "Superman has always meant strength and speed and power—*someone you can count on*. But more, it's a feeling of joy . . . and hope. In what is certainly one of the most ambitious motion picture projects of all time, we are bringing to the screen the most spectacular adventure of all time. Superlatives are bandied around Hollywood much too freely these days, but our film truly *is* movie-making in its grandest sense, with all the ingredients multiplied by a thousand. Everyone will be able to enjoy it and relate to it in some way. Everybody wants to fly, to be free . . . to really be on top of the world—hopefully, a good world."

And so, "Superman"—the movie.

1
The Supermen of Movies

From the "Superman" screenplay, pages 121, 122:

240H EXT. STRATOSPHERE
SUPERMAN climbs higher and higher over the United States, gaining speed, suddenly flings the missile up into space like a javelin. It whistles off into the blackness as SUPERMAN wheels in mid-air, looks back down at the United States, *freezes in horror.*

241 ANGLE ON WESTERN U.S.A.—SUPERMAN'S POV
ROCKET *2 *hits the San Andreas Fault and explodes!* A white-hot *mushroom cloud* starts to form.

241A BACK TO SUPERMAN
SUPERMAN streaks back down to Earth.

241B EXT. SKY—MUSHROOM CLOUD
SUPERMAN circles the mushroom cloud at top speed, going faster and faster, not only stopping its expansion but *actually compressing it.* He then dives straight into the center of the holocaust.

241C INT/EXT. MUSHROOM CLOUD
SUPERMAN swoops to the base of the cloud, *blows upward with his super-breath.*

241D ANGLE ON MUSHROOM CLOUD
The entire cloud with its fallout and pollution is blown *high up into the stratosphere,* away frcm Earth.

242 CLOSE ON SUPERMAN
SUPERMAN stops in mid-air, looks, listens. *A loud rumble begins,* gathering quickly in intensity. *The earthquake has arrived.*

242A EXT. CALIFORNIA COAST—DAY
The land shakes on the Pacific Coast. Huge chunks of cliff begin to fall into the sea.

242B ANGLE ON LANDSCAPE—SUPERMAN'S POV
Great yawning cracks rip open across the land in all directions.

242C ANGLE ON SUPERMAN
SUPERMAN quickly dives down, disappears into a crack in the earth.

•

One thing that spectacular sequence makes clear about "Superman"—it wasn't going to be an ordinary movie. Another is that it was going to be fantastically expensive.

As Marlon Brando, himself one of the major items of expense, put it cheerfully while relaxing on the Shepperton Studios set in April, 1977: "Sure, part of the reason I did it was for the money. But I'm also having one helluva good time."

And while nearly everyone involved was to have doubts about many things in the months to follow, no one on the picture then was inclined to dispute the world's most notable—and, reputedly, often most difficult—film star on either point. Brando's salary for thirteen actual shooting days was reported to be an incredible and unprecedented guarantee of 3.7 million dollars against a percentage of the gross. Of Alexander Salkind's production of "Superman" it has to be said, quite simply, that it stands as the largest, most ambitious motion-picture undertaking ever attempted in the history of films: nearly three years of planning and two of filming; at the height of production employing the full-time talents of more than a thousand people on eleven separate film units; spanning three studios, three continents and eight countries; using well over a million feet of film; and featuring the largest production budget in movie annals.

But as much a part of the "Superman" saga as the fantastic statistics is the constantly startling story of the Herculean challenges and staggering problems, of intrigue and backstage back-stabbing, of incredible bad luck and wild rumors, of dwindling finances, towering talent and clashing personalities, of ambition and avarice and creative idealism—all juxtaposed in a fabulous scenario no film writer could ever have dreamed up.

What warranted this awesome marshaling of ability, effort, time and money, and prompted Warner Brothers to make a multi-million-dollar distribution deal with the producers? For the answer to that, let's, as they say in the movies, zoom in for a close-up on the producers.

•   •   •

Even to dare consider such a prodigious project required inexhaustible imagination and uncanny foresight —attributes that Alexander Salkind, his son Ilya, and

Pierre Spengler seem to have in ample supply. To call them unique would be an understatement.

Second- and third-generation filmmakers, the Salkinds are examples of the new breed of improvisational independent producers who largely control filmmaking today. Alexander Salkind, the "padrone" of the operation, is an elfin figure with a mane of blue-rinsed, snowy hair, a fluent command of six languages and an amazing penchant—even by Hollywood standards—for talking on the telephone. He is also a man with a morbid fear of cats, a claustrophobic antipathy toward airplanes and elevators, and an unrivaled knack for raising millions of dollars.

Trying to get a handle on Alex Salkind isn't easy. Someone who comes close is Maria Monreal, another multilingual, multitalented member of the Salkind team who, over the past five years, has coordinated the distribution of their films, among a myriad of other duties.

"Alex has a one-track mind when it comes to his work," Maria reflected over coffee one morning during the filming, "and he isn't concerned with outside influences. Our print of 'The Three Musketeers' arrived in Beirut just as the violence erupted there a few years ago. Alex only wanted to know *where his film was!* To this day, I think he still holds me responsible for the Lebanese civil war!"

Alex's son Ilya, now thirty, the executive producer, is a chip off the same unorthodox block. Slight of build, like his father, Ilya has a propensity for talking in superlatives, threading small gold chains through his velvet lapels, and writing notes to himself in his black Gucci diary, such as: "Remember me to call Technicolor. And *sound angry!*"

"Basically, my childhood was not, I think, an exciting, normal childhood—it was an exciting, *abnormal* childhood," Ilya said during a quiet moment early in the production. "I was traveling, I traveled all over the world, since I was six months old. So that already gave me a different approach to things. I learned several languages, like my father and mother"—Ilya speaks in a heavily accented English—"which has been enormously helpful. But I also lost a certain sense of reality towards any one country. I was born in Mexico, but I don't know *where* I belong.

"Of course, I had a wonderful time. I was very good-looking, you see. Much better-looking than I am now—no, really, I'm not kidding. I know this might sound vain, but I was good-looking to the extent that things would happen. I didn't even have to *try*.

"Even in my childhood and adolescence, I was very much involved with movies, with my father and grandfather and all. I would go to the movies four or five times a week. Whatever would happen in my life, I would go to the movies. I loved them. I still do."

Producer Pierre Spengler is less flamboyant than Ilya, though possessed of his own colorful aspects—he claims to dream in three languages! A savvy Frenchman with a voracious appetite for work, Spengler grew up on the periphery of the film industry, becoming actively involved through his lifelong friendship with Ilya Salkind. On all their productions, it is Pierre who has overseen the daily operational logistics, while Ilya has concentrated primarily on the casting, promotion and publicity.

And it was Ilya Salkind who first had the idea of launching a major production of "Superman."

●　　　●　　　●

In 1973, the Salkinds and Spengler had their first big hit, a star-studded version of the Dumas classic "The Three Musketeers." Finding themselves with an enormous amount of useable excess footage during the editing of the Richard Lester-directed production, Alex came up with the brilliant scheme of cutting the film in half and releasing it as two different features. And so, with the snip of a scissors, a ready-made sequel, "The Four Musketeers," was in the can. (With "Superman," the producers prudently announced from the outset that two separate films with two separate scripts would be filmed simultaneously, thereby avoiding the outrage provoked by their previous "double feature.") It was an unprecedented stroke of ingenuity, and the distributors and exhibitors, by late '73 already realizing a profit on the first film, were as ecstatic as the producers. Needless to say, the actors were not. When push came to shove, however, they stopped short of court action, for their contracts, the form then standard in the industry, had not in fact specified the number of films they were making. (The two films went on to rack up a combined world-wide gross of $120 million-plus, putting them in the upper ranks of all-time money makers.) The producers are thus inadvertently responsible for the now famous "Salkind clause," an integral part of an actor's contract which states just how many features he or she will be filming at one time.

By the autumn of '73, with the first Musketeer film in release, Ilya Salkind was itching to sink his talents into some new, large-scale production. Walking along the picturesque Avenue Victor-Hugo in Paris one evening, he hit upon a staggering possibility. As he strolled past a local cinema, he observed the one-sheets advertising the current fare, yet another swashbuckling film—"Zorro," the early forties version with Tyrone Power and Basil Rathbone. And then something from Ilya's travels, from those childhood years in New York, clicked in his subconscious. Why not do an all-star, epic-proportion production of America's *ultimate* fictional hero—Superman?

Electrified by enthusiasm, Ilya sped off to the South of France, to Cannes, where Alex was meeting with his financiers. And when Ilya exploded his new film idea,

Alex's reaction was a calm, simple question: "What's 'Superman'?"

After Alex was sufficiently briefed, Ilya called Pierre in Spain, and soon the three producers were huddled at a café, sipping wine and planning their initial strategy. The stage was now set—and "Superman" had taken off.

•   •   •

Ilya and Pierre were eager to talk about the origins of the mammoth "Superman" production. During the early weeks of shooting, they reminisced for hours one afternoon in their modest offices overlooking the formal gardens behind the Pinewood Studios administration block.

"My first reaction to the entire idea was 'It's terrible!,' " Pierre reflected. "I was familiar with the character, though. I knew he was a comic-book hero who could fly and do fantastic feats, and who stood for 'truth, justice and the American way.' That part of it appealed to me. Our films have pretty much always had upbeat messages. But I was very sceptical about *how* to do it, how to approach it. Of course, we all realized the enormous 'camp' potential of the story. And playing up the campiness was one possible approach. But then you would never be able to sustain the story for many years—and by this time, we were already considering sequels. Also, you had to take into account the millions of people all over the world who knew and loved the legend.

"So we all more or less agreed at the outset that if we were to proceed, the only way to do the film was to play it *absolutely straight* and preserve the legend. It was the one way to make it 'believable.' And besides, the humor was there anyway. The thing we wanted to make absolutely certain was that an audience would laugh *with* Superman, never *at* him.

"After Ilya had sold Alex and me on the idea, we had

to convince our traditional backers of the enormous commercial potential of 'Superman.' Most of our money men are European, like us, and I dare say many of them were not really up on American comic-book heroes.

"When we had done this—the merchandising possibilities alone were enough to convince them—we had to track down who owned the rights. And that wasn't too hard to do, either."

"Warner Communications had everything tied up," Ilya joined in, pouring himself an Evian water. "It so happened that 'Superman'—the character—was owned by what was then National Periodical Publications, which was part of the Publishing Division of Warner Communications. So we telephoned our initial overtures from Paris, and, not surprisingly, they didn't take us very seriously. But Alex isn't discouraged easily, and we made a few more calls and soon they started listening. Obviously, the impact of 'Musketeers' was working in our favor.

"They sent one of their top men over, and Alex, Pierre and I had a big meeting in Paris—I think it was August or September of '74. It all went very well, but, of course, it was then that we really got the first inklings of how complex everything was. There were so many areas we had to consider. Naturally, we wanted more than just an option for one picture.

"So many different points had to be discussed, talked about up front," Ilya continued. "They wanted to be sure that we'd be absolutely faithful to the legend. So that meant some kind of script approvals, consultations on casting—you know, things like that. But we had to be careful about protecting ourselves from too much interference in our production. That's why we're independents.

"Anyway, the meetings lasted for three or four days and it didn't look bad—we figured we could iron out the differences. Of course, money was a big problem. They wanted a lot of money, particularly for extended options.

"Well, the Warner rep went back to New York and returned to Europe with a draft of a contract. We re-negotiated a few terms, made a few amendments, and finally he said, 'O.K., if one of you comes to New York for a day, I'll set up a lunch with Bill Sarnoff, Chairman of the Board of Warner Publishing, and you can hassle out any problems and lock everything up.' So Pierre went to New York for that 'day'—and ended up staying for six weeks, during which he negotiated for about ten hours a day, sometimes seven days a week. That should give you an idea of how *big* it was—the potential, I mean. Sarnoff was enormously helpful, and ultimately we hammered out a seventy-five-page contract. A deal acceptable to everyone."

"Basically, it was the mechanics of preserving the integrity of the 'Superman' character that made it all so intricate," Pierre added, "because neither side wanted to give up too much control. Having veto power over selection of the screenwriter, or who would play Superman or Lois Lane, for example—and indeed, lists of names were submitted. But making changes in the production during the shooting is a very hazy area. *We're* the moviemakers and we understand that it's a business that changes from minute to minute, particularly with a production of this size. But then, how do people who are basically publishers in New York City approve things while we're filming four thousand miles away—those little changes that crop up every day? If they send a representative, does he stay on the set at all times? That could make a director uncomfortable. So then, does he approve the rushes? And if he objects to something in the rushes, what then? Particularly if you've just wrapped with a multimillion-dollar star . . . It's all very complicated."

"Anyway," Ilya said, "by now it was late '74 and we still hoped to be in production by some time in '75. So the immediate priorities were to get a first-rate screenplay and director. *And* raise the money."

"Our financing is pretty straightforward," Pierre interjected. "Mostly, we deal with the same core of bankers—Swiss, German, Dutch—whom Alex has developed as 'backers' over the years. Also, by bringing such a massive production to England, we were eligible for what is called 'Eady money,' sort of a system of government matching funds. And this time, we additionally have the major participation of an American bank, the First National Bank of Chicago. So money hasn't been a problem so far."

Pierre smiled, happily unconscious of what lay ahead. Neither he nor the others involved then had any anticipation of the desperate money crunch that would arise in the months to come.

"Getting back to the script," Ilya said, "one of our first choices was William Goldman, who is certainly one of the top screenwriters around today. He was very interested in the project when we approached him, but he was genuinely unclear as to a suitable treatment, so ultimately he said no. Just as high on our list was Mario Puzo. Alex was particularly enthusiastic about Puzo, not only because he thinks Mario is an excellent writer, but also because after a blockbuster like 'The Godfather,' my father also believed that Puzo was exceedingly commercial, that he had a great sense of public tastes and mores. So we approached Puzo, talked, and eventually made him 'an offer he couldn't refuse.'

"So now things seemed to be moving. Mario was supposed to deliver a first draft in April—or was it June?—of '75. Anyway, he submitted a synopsis in April and we thought it had great potential. We even set a production start date of November '75. Of course, that became an impossible date to make.

"Puzo gave us a first-draft screenplay a few months later and a second draft at the beginning of October. It was an incredible script—an amazing achievement, really. The main problem, though, was the considerable length. It was over three hundred pages long—it would have made a six-hour movie! Quite honestly, it was more a *novel* than a screenplay."

The final shooting script of "Superman" incorporates most of Puzo's initial story. There is considerable fascination in reading through the original and seeing what concepts did not make it. In detailing Krypton and its capital city of Kryptonopolis, Puzo casually observed that his vision sounded "expensive, but the city will make at least four or five appearances through the film and justify the cost. . . ." The Puzo script included such camp-sounding characters as JAX-UR, Professor VAKOX and KRU-EL and called for the Elders of Krypton to wear "the futuristic letter 'S' imprinted on their clothes, as does JOR-EL. There should also be a huge futuristic letter 'S' design on the wall of the Council Chamber." Perhaps most intriguing was Puzo's note that "JOR-EL should be played by the same actor as SUPERMAN. Since he is SUPERMAN'S father, this will seem natural. It also gives the star a chance to come into the film right away, rather than wait till we are half an hour into the film." Puzo's suggestion might well have saved the producers some enormous casting problems!

"We took the second draft," Ilya said, "read it carefully, and though we were basically thrilled with the ideas, we felt it needed a few changes and a great deal of editing. We went back to Puzo. By this time, he had thoroughly drained himself on 'Superman' and was already involved in other projects, so he suggested that it might be wiser to get someone else to do the rewrites."

Ilya gave up on the Evian water and mixed Scotch and soda for himself and Pierre. "We then went to one of the top teams in Hollywood, Robert Benton and David and Leslie Newman, writers who had several box office hits like 'Bonnie and Clyde' and 'What's Up, Doc?' to their credit. They basically streamlined the Puzo script and introduced new elements too. But it was still far too long. And there were certain campy features to the script that just didn't fit if we were going to play it a hundred percent straight." (An example of this camp humor occurs on page 37 of the Benton-Newman screenplay. Here Otis, Lex Luthor's oafish henchman, makes his way back to Luthor's subterranean lair by seating himself on a toilet in the men's room of the Plaza Hotel, pulling the flush and then descending—toilet compartment and all—into the depths!)

"Already it was early '76, and we thought we'd be shooting by then," Pierre said. "We took out a full-page ad in *Variety* on February twenty-nine—which, according to the legend, was Superman's actual Leap-year birthday—saying something like 'Happy Birthday, Superman. Sorry we couldn't be with you.' We also arranged for a laser show in Battery Park in New York, where we had a message projected onto a huge balloon by laser beam. I think it was 'Coming soon—Superman the Movie!' I'm pretty sure we were among the first movie producers to employ lasers for publicity like this."

"Anyway," Ilya said, sighing a little, "much later on, when we finally had a director and were ready to shoot, Tom Mankiewicz—he had done several of the big James Bond films—came on as Creative Consultant and really tightened up the screenplay."

"Naturally, as all this was going on, we were in the midst of a search for a director," Pierre continued. "And we wanted a dynamic and imaginative individual with a good track record. Ilya and I had been traveling between Europe and L.A. for months and we both happened to see a movie, 'Sugarland Express,' that didn't make a lot of money but received a good deal of critical attention. We also saw a made-for-TV movie by the same director called 'Duel.' It was also very well done, and the word in Hollywood was that this young guy was going to make it very, very big soon. His name was Steven Spielberg."

Pierre sipped his Scotch and soda. "At this point, 'Jaws,' which Spielberg directed, had already been shot and was being edited. So we called Alex in Europe and said, 'We think this Spielberg is sensational!' And even though Alex had of course never heard of Spielberg, our excitement was enough for him to instruct us to contact Spielberg's agents.

"After a few conversations, it seemed clear that he wanted to do the film. Then he asked for a certain amount of money to direct 'Superman'—a figure which to us seemed high. We got back to Alex and he asked, 'Well, what's he just done? What about his new film?' So we told Alex that the new film was something about a shark and would be coming out in about three or four weeks, and Alex said, 'O.K., let's wait a few weeks to see how this fish movie does.' The rest is more or less history. 'Jaws' came out in June and the initial release made it almost certain that it would become the biggest box-office blockbuster in movie history. Well, Alex flipped out and told us to quickly get back to Spielberg's agent—as if no one else in Hollywood had noticed what was happening to 'Jaws'—but by that time, Spielberg already had a multi-picture package deal with one of the studios. His agent said something about his wanting to do a musical. And the next thing we heard was that 'Close Encounters of the Third Kind' was already in the works with Columbia."

"The story becomes long and frustrating after that," Ilya recalled. "The biggest problem certainly wasn't lack of interest, though. Some people, I think, were honestly afraid of *how* to deal with 'Superman.' We went to just about all the top directors in America. Billy Friedkin was already committed to 'Sorcerer' for Universal. Coppola was at work on 'Apocalypse Now.' And John Guillermin, who had done 'Towering Inferno' a while back, was set for 'King Kong.' So by then we were starting to get worried. We went through most of the list—Robert

Aldrich, Norman Jewison, Arthur Hiller. They were all either involved with some project or just didn't think it was their type of movie. Finally, we went to an Englishman, Guy Hamilton, who had directed some of the biggest and most inventive of the James Bond series, and he was thrilled with the idea and we made a deal. Sadly, we lost him when we switched the picture from Rome to London."

"We *had* planned to do most of the main studio shooting in Cinecittà outside Rome," Pierre continued. "We had begun flying tests in England in early '76, but we already had a production executive—Clive Reed from the 'Musketeers' film—in Rome preparing things: our art director, John Barry, was having sets built, we were crewing up . . . it was all moving. Then *everything* seemed to collapse. Clive became ill and had to bow out of the picture. Another Englishman, Geoffrey Helman, took over, with Bob Simmonds as production supervisor. We were also having union problems in Italy. Most importantly, we realized that nearly all of the special effects we'd be doing would require the top technicians, who would have to be flown in from England anyway. And to add to our problems, we were also in the middle of a multimillion-dollar adaptation of Mark Twain's *The Prince and the Pauper*, which we were shooting in Budapest. So finally Geoffrey suggested that we just shift the entire 'Superman' production to Britain, and we started the negotiations immediately. This was in the autumn of '76."

"Rome had been our choice for a number of practical reasons—economics, facilities, climate," Ilya said. "And we lost a small fortune when we shifted in the midst of pre-production. Hundreds of thousands of dollars worth of sets had already been constructed. As I said, we also lost our director, who's a tax exile from his native Britain. But unquestionably, I think, we gained in the long run by moving the production to England. Without a doubt, we have here the finest craftsmen in the entire film industry. The switch also brought us an *American* director, Dick Donner, which I think we all ultimately realized was essential to 'Superman.' And we finally had a projected start date of March, 1977. Thank God, we all spoke the language, too."

Ilya smiled and continued. "We were at work way before anyone had heard of a 'Star Wars' or a 'Close Encounters of the Third Kind.' We were the first kids on the block to foresee this renewed fascination with science fiction, space and fantasy. It's just taken us a little longer to get it on the screen."

Pierre summed up. "Some people are talking about an undercurrent of resentment in the U.S. because we are European producers who shouldn't be tampering with this sacred part of American folklore. I don't think that's at all true. Quite simply, *we* were the ones who had the idea and initiative and the stamina to put this film together. And rather than tampering with anything, our first goal has always been to make an entertaining movie that totally upholds the legend. That's why we put Americans in all the key cast and crew positions. Anyway, what *is* an American? America is a nation of immigrants, the best of Europe and the world. I think people all over will be glad that someone finally made this into a feature film."

•   •   •

I started doing research for this book in October, 1975, happy with the prospect of writing about a subject on which one could quote both Nietzsche and Rona Barrett. I was given free rein to write, record, interview and inspect every aspect of the film, good or bad, which I felt might be of interest to moviegoers and readers all over the world.

As I worked, the producers went on struggling to get their vision before a camera. By January of 1977, they had weathered the criticism, overcome the enormous odds, and assembled an international production of mammoth proportions.

The only thing missing was . . . SUPERMAN.

2
Superstars

Perhaps the greatest problem in casting the title role of
"Superman" was the basic fact that after forty years,
every one of the millions of comic-book fans had his
own idea of exactly how Superman should look. Certainly, the Salkinds and Spengler—and, eventually,
Warner Brothers—were sharply mindful of just how important "looking the part" would be. They all recalled
how the hugely successful James Bond series almost
collapsed when Sean Connery vacated the part. Whoever was cast as Superman would have to look like
Superman.

And, of course, he'd have to be able to act. The role
was a demanding one, admittedly one of the best potential star vehicles of the past ten years, and in a production that was promising to become one of the most important movies ever made, Alex Salkind wanted to be
sure he'd have more on the screen than a mass of muscle
who happened to look like a comic-book hero. And he
wanted a superstar in the title role.

The producers began their quest for a Superman early
in 1975. The search didn't end until a press conference
at Sardi's in New York on February 23, 1977—one month
and five days before shooting began!

The senior Salkind's first choice for the part was America's number-one box-office heart-throb, Robert Redford.
Satisfied with him as an actor, Alex believed that with

the right make-up, the blond, blue-eyed Redford would look "Supermannish" enough to carry the part off. And his world-wide popularity would be a definite plus with Salkind's backers as well as with potential distributors. But the initial overtures bogged down because of money demands and the lack of a finished script, and eventually Redford turned down the part. Though Alex was momentarily disappointed, it wasn't too long—though it was long before the part was cast—before all three producers realized the wisdom of that decision. As one well-known American agent remarked, "Redford would have been playing *Redford playing Superman.* After all, who would have believed *him* flying around in a blue leotard and red booties?"

After Redford's refusal, Ilya Salkind took on his usual casting responsibilities, leaving the financing and other pre-production matters to his father and Pierre Spengler. Ilya also enlisted the considerable talents of Lynn Stalmaster, Hollywood's top casting agent, to aid in the search for a suitable Superman. Mary Selway, one of Britain's foremost casting directors, came onto the picture much later to assist with casting in the U.K.

The next top star toward whom Ilya turned was veteran actor Paul Newman. Though the three producers had expressed their separate doubts about the fifty-two-year-old Newman playing a thirtyish Man of Steel, Salkind sent him a copy of the script, then in its first revision, with instructions that he could negotiate for either of two main roles, Superman or Lex Luthor. In the end, Newman turned down both.

"I think the unfinished status of the script had a lot to do with it," Ilya reflected later. "And I guess our own confusion and uncertainties didn't help, either."

After Newman, it became a free-for-all. Between Ilya's own hunches and Stalmaster's suggestions, the producers and other key people involved saw well over two hundred would-be Supermen during the next eighteen months, ranging from the top of the Hollywood firmament to professional athletes, unknown beachcombers, Austrian weightlifters—and even a Beverly Hills dentist! And all the while, the gossip columns in the "trades" and the booths in the Polo Lounge were buzzing about who had just landed the super role of the seventies. Scarcely a week went by without either Army Archerd in *Daily Variety* or Hank Grant in the *Hollywood Reporter* "leaking" the news that "wunderkind producer Ilya Salkind has definitely decided on (so-and-so) to star as Superman."

On into '76, the roster of possible stars included Steve McQueen ("too heavy"), Clint Eastwood ("too busy"), Charles Bronson ("too earthy") and Sylvester Stallone ("too Italian"). Nick Nolte, Burt Reynolds, James Caan, Ryan O'Neal, Jon Voight and Sam Elliott were also high on a list that included John Beck, Perry King, Jeff Bridges, Jan-Michael Vincent, David Soul, Robert Wagner, Paul Rudd, Lyle Waggoner and Kris Kristofferson! But still, no Superman.

By early summer of '76, with "The Prince and the Pauper" (released in the States as "Crossed Swords") in production and a possible late autumn start date looming for "Superman" in Rome, the pressure to fill the title role became intense. (Perhaps the producers took some solace in the knowledge that "Gone With the Wind" had actually begun shooting without Scarlett!) Some of the Hollywood rumors had already started to turn sour; there was talk that the Salkinds were unable to secure a suitable Superman and the picture was about to collapse. Even in Europe, little of this negative chatter was lost on Alexander Salkind's banking connections.

So the producers—having spent a great deal of time, effort and money, and having listened to hours of conflicting advice—now decided to change their original tactic and go after a superstar of the first magnitude to play one of the principal *supporting* roles in "Superman" —Jor-El, the Man of Steel's father. And there was unanimous agreement that only *one* actor had the appropriate stature and talent—Marlon Brando.

Brando was still at work on Francis Ford Coppola's beleaguered production of "Apocalypse Now," being shot under incredibly difficult conditions in the Phillippines. So the Salkinds made their first proposal through long-time family friend and super agent Kurt Frings. Frings, a legendary fixture on the Hollywood scene, submitted the offer to Brando in mid-June and after only two weeks of negotiations, the biggest acting deal in movie history had been clinched.

"I wasn't really Marlon's adviser. I was more a liaison with the Salkinds. In other words, I was more or less working with the Salkinds to try and get Marlon to do the picture," Frings has explained. "Marlon said that the price was too good to turn down. Nearly four million dollars—the highest salary ever!"

Brando's involvement gave the production a stamp of approval and authority, definitely letting the world know that this wasn't going to be some "cartoon" picture. It certainly quieted the muckrakers in the industry. And it seemed to be enough for the Salkinds' backers.

"When producers pay what appears to be an astronomical sum of money to an actor, the public usually points an accusing finger, as if we were some kind of profligate schmucks who don't know what we're doing," Ilya explained after concluding the Brando deal. "Sure, we realize the old star system is dead. Very few people go to a movie just to see a favorite actor or actress. It's more a writer's industry now. But a new star system of sorts does exist. There are certain actors and actresses we refer to as 'bankable'—just by signing them, you can put an entire picture together. They also give you the clout to talk with the 'majors'—the principal distributors. A name can start the ball rolling—*and* keep the money flowing."

With Brando set to play Jor-El, the producers had a

little leeway in their search for Superman. And, watching television highlights of the 1976 summer Olympic games from Munich (there wasn't much else to do at night in Budapest, where "The Prince and the Pauper" was filming), Ilya and Pierre were greatly impressed—along with the rest of the world—by the achievements of a handsome American decathlon gold medalist, Bruce Jenner.

Now that the producers had their first superstar (Gene Hackman, accepting two million dollars to play the evil genius, Lex Luthor, became the scecond), they were prepared to consider the possibility of going with a total newcomer in the title role. And Bruce Jenner, with his dark hair, blue eyes and boyish good looks, seemed a very hot prospect. Besides, he had openly expressed his interest in launching a career in films. The question was, could he act?

In September, after "The Prince and the Pauper" was in the can, Jenner was flown to Rome, given a screen test . . . and was rejected by the three filmmakers "because he appeared much too young on the screen." Some of the production staffers working at Cincecittà at the time, however, were more blunt. "I think, quite simply, it boiled down to that fact that Jenner is *not* an actor," one of the technicians revealed. "He looked good. It's just that he lacked that assurance that comes with experience."

So out went the idea of a professional athlete, and a dejected Ilya Salkind flew back to the States to interview more candidates. The producers also thought it a good idea to put the kibosh on stories circulating in Hollywood that had engaging muscleman Arnold Schwarzenegger halfway to Krypton!

By early December, "Superman" had shifted to Shepperton Studios outside London. Guy Hamilton had exited the picture and the American Dick Donner had had taken over as director. In New York, Donner and the younger Salkind closeted themselves in the Sherry-

Netherland Hotel to interview another phalanx of Superman hopefuls.

After days of no luck, a desperate Ilya started poring over the voluminous Academy Players Directory (a compendium of Screen Actors Guild-registered players) and came across a photo next to which he had, months ago, scribbled some of his inimitable chicken-scratches. It was someone Stalmaster had mentioned back then; a twenty-four-year-old local actor with a considerable list of theatrical and television credits. Ilya decided to call Christopher Reeve and invite him to come chat with Donner and himself.

The six-foot four-inch, 180-pound Reeve—no relation to the TV Superman, George Reeves—arrived looking drawn and perhaps a little too lanky. He had recently returned from California and a part in "Gray Lady Down" with Charlton Heston, and was currently playing each night opposite Katharine Hepburn in Enid Bagnold's "A Matter of Gravity" on Broadway.

The three men chatted at length—about "everything *but* 'Superman,'" Ilya later remembered—but Dick Donner seemed basically unimpressed. He thought Chris was just too young and too skinny, though obviously he was handsome, intelligent and talented. Anyway, the cautious Donner was still inclined to opt for a big-name star. Salkind, however, was enthusiastic, especially after they had persuaded Chris to put on a pair of horn-rimmed glasses and adopt a Clark Kent-ish mien.

Back in Hollywood, this time locked away at the Salkinds' bungalow on the grounds of the Beverly Hills Hotel, the director and producer spent a depressing holiday season sipping stale cups of coffee and seeing an endless stream of would-be Supermen.

With a tentative start date of March '77 at Shepperton, the exhausted filmmakers became desperate in their search for a Man of Steel. "We kept moaning to each other, 'Why can't things ever happen like they do in the movies? Why can't someone just walk in that door and *be* Superman? Someone like Clark Gable or Gary Cooper!'" Ilya recalls with a grimace of pain. "So then one day my wife Skye Aubrey"—the actress daughter of former CBS and MGM mogul James T. Aubrey, Jr.— "came in, enthusing, 'Hey, I've got this terrific guy, Don . . . he's my *dentist* . . . seriously . . . and I think he looks just like Superman. Even Ryan O'Neal told Don he looked right for the role, since you don't want Ryan anyway. So what do you think?' Well, needless to say, Dick and I thought perhaps this dentist was a bit too free with the sodium pentothal or something. We certainly didn't feel inclined to waste another hour with some Beverly Hills dentist. But then I said, 'Maybe I could kill two birds with one stone and have my teeth cleaned at the same time!' I don't think Skye appreciated that.

"Anyway, I figured we had nothing to lose but a little more time and we were really beginning to panic. So despite Dick's reluctance—I guess he thought I'd gone bananas—we took Skye's advice and called the guy, a well-known Beverly Hills dentist named Don Voyne, and then came that knock at the door—and wham! In walked Superman! Dick and I both thought this Voyne was great. Turns out he was something of a physical-fitness fanatic—tennis, jogging—like most Californians. So we arranged for a screen test at Shepperton in January, and Dick and I flew back to London, confident that we had our star.

"Well, we put Voyne in a Superman suit and ran the test. And in a complete turn-around from Jenner's test, he just looked too old. I mean, he's a very good-looking guy—in his mid-thirties, I guess—but he didn't convey that youth and power and courage that you associate with Superman. We all realized it at that moment. I don't know, maybe he could have pulled it off by strong direction, but there was no guarantee."

So at that point, with the start of shooting less than eight weeks away, a frantic Ilya Salkind went back to

Donner and persuaded him to schedule a proper screen test at the studio for the New York actor who had so impressed the producer.

Salkind vividly recalls the persistent doubts of his director. "Dick kept insisting that Chris was too young—and Pierre was inclined to agree, judging from the photographs—but I reminded them both that we had options for seven, possibly ten, 'Superman' movies and a relative newcomer would probably be more believable to audiences and would grow into the part."

When Reeve arrived in London, he was met at the airport by Spengler's attractive French wife Monique, who was on her way to the studio for lunch. And her intuitive reaction, conveyed to her husband as soon as she arrived, was that Chris was a knockout. However, Donner's concern that Chris was too young and too thin wasn't assuaged by the reaction of one woman.

All that changed with Reeve's screen test. As Clark Kent—in gray flannel suit and black wing-tip shoes, with slicked-down hair and glasses—Chris's characterization of the mild-mannered reporter was a tour de force, with just the right balance of sincerity and "klutziness." And as Superman, there was the total transformation so crucial to the part—and the success of the film. Dramatically lit, with professional make-up and a little padding, Reeve cut an undeniably striking figure as the Man of Steel. He certainly didn't look too young *or* too skinny. In fact, he virtually exploded on the screen.

The producers had considered hundreds of possibilities, seen hundreds more, and had actually tested ten. Now they felt they had their man. But still they waited to make their decision known.

Traveling back to Heathrow Airport with an uncertain Chris Reeve in the back seat, studio driver Bunny Barkus, a jovial Englishman with a flair for hunches, assured his nervous passenger, "I've seen nearly the whole lot of 'em . . . and *you've* got the part!"

Chris went back to New York and a near-normal life —until his manager called early one morning in February, shrieking that he'd just heard Rona Barrett announce on ABC's "Good Morning, America" that Chris had been chosen to play Superman. And a phone call from Salkind had confirmed the story.

"A very distinct advantage and a consideration in casting someone like Chris," Ilya told me soon after Reeve's choice had been made public, "is that apart from the talent and physical appearance, an actor who isn't established in films is much more amenable to negotiating for several options. That isn't so easy with a million-dollar superstar. And after all, we do plan to make several 'Superman' movies.

"We're paying Chris a good salary for someone just launching a motion-picture career. We wanted him to *feel* like a star, to be able to stay in the fast track. And don't forget, his salary has an escalator clause for each additional picture!"

Thinking back on that all-important decision, Chris Reeve was realistically blunt in appraising how an almost unknown stage actor was cast in one of the best parts in film history:

"I think it was basically because they had to have someone who could look like the public's idea of the comic-magazine character. And that is a very precise image which has existed for forty years. So the producers had the responsibility of taking the image the public had known for all that time, and then they had to 'modernize' it, bring it up to date with the seventies, because the public conception of the character has, of course, been influenced by the George Reeves television series of the fifties.

"I think that I was a pretty good compromise, that I *do*—once the make-up and stuff is complete—look like the guy in the comics. And yet, I also look like a man of the seventies, rather than a fifties person. So the reason I was selected was that I answered a very specific physical description.

"The rest of it . . . well, of course they needed a good actor too. But the public reaction on that score, I think, is fairly low. People are assuming that the actor who plays Superman really doesn't matter, as long as you have somebody who *looks* the part—the stars in the movie will carry the weight. You know, Marlon Brando, Gene Hackman and everybody else, they'll pull it through. And I think the producers would have settled for that. What I'm trying to do is give them more than they expected. So I've treated the film like I would treat being in a Broadway play. I've treated it as seriously as anything I've done. In other words, I'm not going along for the ride . . . I'm not going to sit back and let other people do everything for me in the movie."

With the title role finally filled, an enthusiastic Dick Donner ordered Reeve, who had just returned to London, to adopt a radical regimen that would transform his lanky physique into something more befitting the kid from Krypton. Reeve embarked on a carefully structured routine that included pumping iron at the Grosvenor House gym with former British body-building champ David Prowse (better known as Darth Vader of "Star Wars"), an extra meal every day, protein milkshakes and a rainbow of vitamins. The sensitive and somewhat vulnerable-looking Reeve was on his way to becoming a picture-perfect specimen of rock-hard musculature.

For the moment, things seemed to be progressing according to schedule. Just barely.

•　　•　　•

Now that Superman had been set, the producers' most immediate task was finding a Lois Lane to play opposite him. Almost as soon as the euphoria over Reeve had subsided, panic set in again. Shooting was less than four weeks away, and most of the major roles, including Lois, were yet to be cast.

Just why was Ilya Salkind so flagrantly late in finding the right people for each part?

"Because he's incredibly disorganized, that's why!" Pierre assured me during one of our lengthy chats.

"Yes," Ilya agreed. "Things like that happen for a very simple reason . . . I *am* incredibly disorganized!" He smiled impishly. "No, honestly, the reason is that all our efforts were focused on finding a Superman. I knew we had to find him first. *Then* we'd have to find a Lois Lane to complement him. Look, I firmly believe that with such an enormous film, with so many influences changing all the time and new elements always coming up, the later you cast, the better. First of all, on a picture this size, the schedule is being altered continually, which affects the availability of certain big stars. Also, since changes in the script are ongoing—and with this movie, that's been the rule, not the exception—you find that someone you originally thought would be great for a part as it was first conceived turns out to be totally inappropriate. I don't say that this policy is logical or that it works for everyone all the time, but it has usually worked for me."

While the search went on for Lois, British casting agent Mary Selway was hard at work filling a number of major and minor roles with distinguished international —though mainly English—stars.

Stage and screen actress Susannah York was set to play opposite Brando as Superman's Krytonian mother, Lara, after names like Anne Bancroft and Joanne Woodward had been considered. Some criticism popped up in the American press about the casting of an Englishwoman to play America's "supermom." But the decision of the writers, as well as of the producers and director, was to establish a universal tone for the picture, particularly with regard to an out-of-this-world setting like the planet Krypton. Also, it was good politics on the part of the producers, since the flow of matching funds from the British government depended in part on the use of English actors and actresses in key roles—something that almost stopped the picture at a later date.

Terence Stamp was cast to play Superman's arch-nemesis, General Zod; rising English star Sarah Douglas was set as Ursa, Zod's female accomplice in evil; and six-foot six-inch, 250-pound American former pro boxer Jack O'Halloran rounded out the terrible trio as the bestial Non.

For the relatively minor roles of members of Krypton's Council of Elders, Mary Selway still sought to cast only the most distinguished and accomplished artists. And, in fact, she had little trouble in securing such veteran British film stars as Harry Andrews and Trevor Howard for a growing roster of performers that read like a *Who's Who* of films. Maria Schell, Austrian-born star of numerous internationally acclaimed motion pictures, agreed to play Vond-Ah, a Kryptonian scientist and one of Jor-El's chief accusers. And in two major casting coups, Valerie Perrine and Academy Award nominee Ned Beatty were signed for the starring roles of the voluptuous villainess Eve Teschmacher and Lex Luthor's bungling henchman, Otis.

This flurry of casting continued to generate pre-production publicity for "Superman." It also served to heighten the speculation as to who would cop what *Newsweek* was calling one of the "best female leads of the decade."

•   •   •

Now it was March, and Salkind and Spengler put their search for Lois into high gear. Ilya's office was soon flooded with photos, resumes and agents' phone calls on behalf of ingenue starlets. But, as with Superman, there was a very specific concept that the producers and director had for their Lois: liberated, hard-nosed, witty, and of course, attractive.

Before long, there was a steady stream of stars flying both ways across the Atlantic, and screen tests were scheduled at Shepperton with very few hours allowed for jet lag. Barbara Streisand was considered and the idea immediately abandoned, since everyone agreed that she was wrong for the part—also, it was doubtful that someone of her superstar status would have submitted to the formality of the screen test Donner insisted upon. "King Kong" heroine Jessica Lange was also crossed off as not being quite what they were looking for. Jill Clayburgh, sassy star of "Gable and Lombard" and "Silver Streak," was unavailable. Other names that were considered, pursued or rejected included Liza Minnelli, Shirley MacLaine, Natalie Wood and Christina Raines. Someone even mentioned Carrie Fisher, who had made such an impact in "Shampoo" and who had recently completed a starring role in what some film people were saying might be a great sleeper—"Star Wars."

All through March and on into April, tests were held —opposite Chris Reeve—for people like Deborah Raffin, Susan Blakely, Stockard Channing and Leslie Ann Warren. For a while, it looked as though Warren was the choice. She fit the description, and since she was not widely known, the odds were that she wouldn't overshadow Chris. Still, Donner and the producers hesitated.

Back in Los Angeles, the director and writer Tom Mankiewicz held script meetings and continued to search. Finally they decided to contact a young actress whose work they had admired and whose talent, they felt, had been largely overlooked. They telephoned Margot Kidder—she was on her Montana ranch with her husband, writer Tom McGuane, and her infant daughter —and told her to come to Los Angeles to read for the part of Lois Lane in "Superman."

"When Tom called, frankly, I thought, 'What *is* this,

some kind of a joke or something?'" Margot told me between takes one day. "But then I flew down to L.A. and read the script and I flipped. I loved it! After I read, they said 'Good . . . great!,' but I really didn't think they were being honest. I was too nervous and scared. But then they asked me, 'Look, can you stick around?' and I said 'No, I have to get back home to Montana right away.' So they looked at me a little weird and assured me, 'Oh, well, we'll call you over the weekend.' Yeah, well, I'd heard *that* before. And when I didn't get a call from them I figured they didn't want me. Then on Monday they telephoned and asked me to fly to London in *two days* for a screen test!"

In England, Margot tested and then sat and chain-smoked for two more days, awaiting the decision. The waiting was worth it. She had the part.

"It was all terribly flattering," Margot gushed. "I didn't really think of it as the 'top female lead' until I read it! My first reaction was, 'Thank God, I really need the money!' Then I went out to the best lingerie boutique on Beauchamp Place in London and bought six hundred bucks' worth of underwear!

"I never read a 'Superman' comic until the day before my screen test—my stepson gave me his comic. So I think that most of what I bring to the role of Lois is myself. I'm manic and I'm overambitious, and I'm often frantic and disorganized. I always think I'm being highly efficient when actually I'm not. And that seems to be a part of what Dick Donner wants. The calm side of me belongs in another movie."

•   •   •

With the "above-the-title" roles and most of the other major parts cast, the entire "Superman" production office was frantically dealing with the last-minute odds and ends of pre-production: making sure sets were in order, double checking on quantities of 35mm film stock, putting finishing stitches in costumes, typing out insurance forms and, of course, filling the hundreds of technical positions on the massive "Superman" crew. For, of course, the only way to complement a superstar cast was with a superstar crew.

3
Some Good Omens...
Dick Donner...
and England

"Only two people could have directed 'Superman,'"
award-winning camera operator Peter MacDonald assured me—I hope not too tongue-in-cheek—"and *both* of
them are Dick Donner!"

That is not a bad snap assessment of Richard Donner,
a man whose frenetic enthusiasm, energy and imagination carried the movie through some of the darkest days
of production.

From the moment a film starts shooting, it becomes—
at least in theory—the director's picture. ("From your
mouth to God's ears," Donner confided to me during
our first chat at Shepperton.) So it was a foregone con-
clusion that with a film as monumental and potentially
problematical as "Superman," Donner wouldn't always
be in the tranquil eye of the swirling storm. In fact, on
many occasions, he was the whole damn tornado!

When Guy Hamilton departed from the picture in
late 1976, the producers had to find a replacement, a
director with the temperament and track record to cope
with a production like "Superman," and someone they
could sell to their moneymen—preferably an American.

Both Ilya and Pierre had been impressed by a relatively low-budget film with a high-budget look that had
been released earlier in the year and had racked up
enough box-office receipts to become a top money-maker.
So they screened "The Omen" for Alex Salkind and a

collective decision was made to approach the director, Richard Donner.

Late one Sunday evening, Donner received a trans-atlantic telephone call in Los Angeles from a man with a funny accent: "This is Alexander Salkind. Do you know who I am?" When Donner replied in the negative, Alex continued, "Well, I'm the producer of 'Superman' and I saw 'The Omen' and I'd like you to direct my film.".

Wham! Just like that.

Donner was flattered . . . and somewhat stunned. Most of the forty-seven-year-old director's experience was in American television, on which he had launched both the "Kojak" and "Bronk" series and directed one of the most successful made-for-television movies, "Sarah T.— Portrait of a Teenage Alcoholic" with Linda Blair. His credits in feature films—"X-15" with Charles Bronson, "Salt and Pepper" with Sammy Davis Jr. and Peter Lawford, and "Twinky" with Bronson and Susan George, the latter two directed in England—were more modestly successful. But "The Omen" had achieved that elusive blockbuster status, and now Donner was one of the hottest directors in Hollywood.

Donner told the senior Salkind that he would like to read the "Superman" script. When he did, he turned the film down. "I told them there was specific things in the script that had to be changed, and I would be willing to direct if I could rewrite the screenplay. Understand-ably, they were reluctant to talk about rewrites, since the script had already undergone several transformations. But I was adamant—I thought the script was getting too far away from Puzo's original concept, which was ex-cellent—and so it looked as if that would be the end of it. However, we got back to each other, decided to meet in Paris, and agreed to bring Tom Mankiewicz in to do the revisions. So I accepted the Salkinds' offer and we were on our way."

Tom Mankiewicz has a humorous footnote to Donner's

acceptance of the offer to direct "Superman." Tom told me, "When Dick was already about ninety percent sure of doing the picture, to save crucial time at that late date the costume department sent him several swatches of materials being considered for Chris's Superman costume. They wanted to make sure the colors would be right for all the matte shots and that the textures would be good for the flying. Well, they also sent along one of the complete Superman uniforms—cape and all—that I guess had been made up a while back for Guy Hamilton's O.K. Anyway, Dick calls me up one night— he was still wrestling with his decision and I think he must have had a few drinks or something—and he says 'Tom, I went upstairs and I put that costume on, the whole thing, and that's it. Something's come over me and I've made up my mind, damn it! I'm hooked!' And that was that."

I asked Donner if he was at all intimidated by the knowledge that he had not been the producers' first choice as director.

"Not at all," he assured me. "I only wish I had been involved earlier so that I would have had more time to prepare. Preparation time is vital on any film, even more so on an enormous undertaking like this. But if you have faith in a picture, you should be flattered that you were called, no matter when."

As an American, long familiar with the legend and the character, what perspective and interpretation would he bring to "Superman"?

"Both Mankiewicz and I decided that we would treat the picture as reality . . . 'larger than life,' but still reality. This was in perfect keeping with the producers' viewpoint. The key to the whole concept of the film is *verisimilitude*." Donner pointed to the wall behind his desk, where the key word was emblazoned in large letters. "We've treated it as truth. And the minute you are unfaithful to the truth . . . to the dignity of the legend . . . the minute you screw around with it or make fun of it or parody it and make it into a spoof, then you destroy its innocence and honesty.

"None of us are being pretentious about it. We know we're dealing with a comic-magazine character. But the main aim of our interpretation is to uphold and enhance a great American myth—it"s part of our tradition. Of course, there'll be humor. Of course audiences will laugh and say 'Oh, come on!' when they hear familiar catch phrases like 'mild-mannered reporter.' But that's just what everyone *expects*. That's all in keeping with the verisimilitude of the legend. It's real within its own framework."

What about his responsibility for the ultimate success or failure of the film?

"Look," Donner replied without hesitation, "as the sages say, 'A director is only as good as his last picture.' Well, I live or die by my films. If it's a hit, the producers can take the credit—along with everybody else. If it's a flop, it's the director's fault. That's always the way.

"Anyway, when producers hire a director, they must have faith in him, because they allocate to *him* the authority to make their movie. If the producers *don't* have that faith, then they shouldn't hire him. I'm not worried, though. We've got the best people working on this film. Our Superman is the most disciplined, in-volved, totally committed young actor I've ever worked with. He's fantastic. And three days after this picture comes out, his face is going to be plastered on the bedroom wall of every chick in the world. And we've cer-tainly got one of the best damn crews that's ever been assembled. So, no, I'm not worried."

•   •   •

Not many in the picture business were likely to challenge Donner's evaluation of the "Superman" crew, which the producers, their production executives and then the late-arriving director had so carefully recruited.

British film crews had become highly sought after, and such big-budget American movies as "Star Wars," "A Bridge Too Far" and "The Deep" had been largely staffed by English men and women. Certainly the economic benefits of filming in the United Kingdom and the Commonwealth provided an attractive incentive for the producers of all these films, as well as for the producers of "Superman." But the long tradition of craftsmanship, effort and ability which still prevails in the British film business was probably the decisive factor in shifting the production from Rome to London.

Many of the crew had come from "Star Wars" and "A Bridge Too Far," two of the most important films of 1977. (David Tomblin, the burly, bearlike first assistant director, came from the latter production and had also worked with Donner on "The Omen.") As director of photography, the producers had hired Geoffrey Unsworth, unquestionably one of the most distinguished in the world. Winner of an Academy Award for "Cabaret," Unsworth came to "Superman" with his equally notable camera team of many years: camera operator Peter MacDonald, focus puller John Campbell, and clapper-loader Steve Barron.

The "Superman" art department boasted the talents of production designer John Barry and his assistants, art director Norman Reynolds, Norman Dorme and Les Dilley, all except Dorme veterans of the film everyone was talking about, "Star Wars" (for which Barry, Reynolds and Dilley won a 1977 Academy Award).

Costume designer Yvonne Blake had to her credit such films as "Jesus Christ Superstar," both "Musketeer" pictures, and "Robin and Marian," and she had won an Oscar for the lavish "Nicholas and Alexandra."

Other "Star Wars" alumni included the make-up and hairdressing artists. Stuart and Kay Freeborn, along with their son Graham, were responsible for the outrageously imaginative creatures in "Star Wars" and for the ape-man creatures in Stanley Kubrick's "2001." Hairdresser Pate McDermott—fragile-looking, soft-spoken, with a lilting Irish accent—had, often, "Star Wars," recently completed work on Peter Yates' production of "The Deep."

The sound department was headed by veteran mixer Roy Charman, a puckish, good-natured fellow who, along with boom operator George Rice and his assistant Mike Tucker, had done "The Prince and the Pauper" and several other Salkind productions.

Of all the hundreds of special effects planned for "Superman," clearly the most important was flying. And the producers and Donner had put together a superb unit. Guided by Wally Veevers, who would handle the special "process projection" systems required, the flying unit included Denys Coop, Dominic Fulford, Derek Botell and special editor Ernie Walters, experienced veterans of films like "2001," "The Day of the Jackal," "The Man Who Would Be King," "A Bridge Too Far" and "Star Wars." And to execute the flying sequences, along with Chris Reeve himself, top men like Alf Joint, Vic Armstrong and Paul Weston of Stunts Inc. had been lined up.

Mechanical special effects—breakaways, buildings collapsing, helicopters crashing, cars running amok and the like—were largely the responsibility of Colin Chilvers (at Pinewood) and John Richardson (on the North American locations).

Equally important to the effects on a film like "Superman" was the model unit—eventually the film would have two—in charge of everything from creating scaled-down versions of the Man of Steel himself to constructing entire mini-cities and planets. Under the skillful direction of Derek Meddings, with Paul Wilson as cameraman and Les Bowie overseeing the matte and model construction, the "Superman" model units would shoot some of the most ambitious, detailed and delicate model sequences ever envisioned, using many techniques that had never been employed before.

Whatever couldn't be achieved by the other "effects" teams would usually fall under the purview of the optical department, headed by expert Roy Field. Roy had been hired by the producers long before the film was scheduled to start shooting, giving him time to study the script and decide just what kind of opticals—dissolves, fades, superimpositions—would be needed. The task would indeed be a considerable one: some 365 optical shots were required to create the fantastic visual impact of "Star Wars"—and "Superman" would require *at least* 100 more.

One of England's top continuity women, Elaine Schreyeck, was assigned to keep daily track of all the details during the shooting, guiding Dick and everyone else by making sure Chris's cloak was flapping in the right direction or that Valerie Perrine's penciled beauty marks didn't suddenly move around her face from one scene to the next. The always decorous and dignified Schreyeck soon became a familiar figure around the studio, pedaling her bicycle between sound stages, her big bulging clipboards strapped neatly behind her.

Since all of this effort would eventually result in a million-plus feet of celluloid, it would be the ongoing job of editor Stuart Baird to assemble it into a full-length feature film. Baird, a wraithlike "workaholic" of Scots descent and one of Britain's youngest and most accomplished editors, had been a protégé of Lindsey Anderson and Ken Russell. He had edited Donner's smash "The Omen" and now, with his assistants Bob Mullen, David Beesley, Mike Duthie and Neal Farrell, he looked forward to working with the director again on this mammoth undertaking.

To let everyone in the world know that "Superman" was being made into a movie—without being too blatant about it—Ilya Salkind hired as publicists the low-keyed, even-tempered and eminently English Gorden Arnell and his equally unflappable assistant June Broom. Arnell in turn brought in a documentary film crew and still photographer Bob Penn. Penn, a good-natured, easy-going chap, drives a Rolls Silver Shadow, and takes incredibly beautiful photographs—his work has graced eight *Life* magazine covers. And I owe Bob a special debt of thanks for his pictures in this book.

At the heart of this army of employees was the unit office, coordinated by unit manager Dusty Symonds and production assistant Pat Carr, who did everything from typing daily progress reports and ordering equipment to regulating the flow of studio transport.

By mid-March, fully crewed with several hundred production staffers—film technicians; make-up, hairdressing and wardrobe people; carpenters, painters, plasterers, electricians and riggers; extraes, stand-ins, stuntmen; doctors, nurses, drivers—"Superman" was finally ready to take off.

•　　•　　•

It is difficult—and perhaps patronizing—for a foreigner to comment on another country's national character, but it's clear to me that a typically British spirit of enthusiasm, doggedness and pride in craftsmanship infused our crew—that peculiar amalgam that produced Shakespeare, the Battle of Britain airmen, and the Sex Pistols. I can't help feeling that this idiosyncratic "Englishness" accounted in large part for the energy and excellence of the film.

Though moods would change and enthusiasm often flag in the long and difficult months ahead, that spirit was much in evidence when the cameras started rolling on "A" Stage at Shepperton Studios on Monday, March 28, 1977.

4
"In the beginning....": Brando

As if anticipating the mixture of emotions and events in store for "Superman," the weather in England on the first day of principal photography was a potpourri of sunshine, blustery winds, rain and snow.

I was up at 6:30 that morning to hitch a lift with Ilya Salkind's driver, Ron Jackson, from my studio flat in the Kensington Hilton for the thirty-odd-mile commute to Shepperton. Shooting would start promptly at 8:30, as it would most days, and like everyone else, I was anxious to see one of motion pictures' true living legends in action.

Strictly speaking, "Superman" had actually begun filming almost a year earlier, with trial runs on the flying, performers' tests, and some background plate shots. But March 28 was the first full day of main unit shooting. *And* the first day of Brando.

When I arrived at Shepperton, my initial goal was to get my bearings and meet the cast, crew and production personnel who would be a part of my life for the next year or more.

Shepperton is a small studio by Hollywood standards. Dating back to the more prosperous days of the British film industry, it is today a "four-wall" setup—they simply rent out space and each production brings in its own staff and equipment. Recently, most of Shepperton was bought by the popular British rock group, The Who, to be used as a recording studio.

After making the rounds, I stopped by the production office, where I was assigned to an office in the "Old House" (the original tenant's mansion, now the administration block) and given a copy of what is every film production's daily battle plan, the call sheet.

The call sheet is based on the far more elaborate master shooting schedule, which is arranged weeks, even months, in advance by the producers, the director and the production staff. *Supposedly* the entire production is mapped out from the first day of filming to the moment the picture wraps. I emphasize "supposedly" because film schedules are rarely realistic and must be constantly amended, and "Superman" turned out to be no exception to this rule. The call sheet tells everyone on a daily basis *who* (Chris Reeve, Dick Donner, ten extras) should be *where* (C stage, back lot, in make-up, on East 57th Street) *when* (6:30 A.M., 8:30 A.M., 5:30 P.M.) and with *what* (a pair of glasses, a bottle of wine, a dummy baby, 3 green kryptonite crystals). After several years of working in or around feature films, it has never ceased to amaze me that someone, somewhere, actually sits down and works out the logistical nightmare of all these details—an incredibly intricate task, particularly with a production the size of this one.

•　　•　　•

Ever since Marlon Brando's arrival date had been leaked to the London press, the local papers, along with wire service journalists from all over the world, had been running stories about the superstar, ranging from his "astronomical" salary (one publication had him getting $40 million for a week's work, apparently confusing his fee with the total production budget) to his overweight problem (a trade journal claimed he was tipping the scales at nearly three hundred pounds).

Ignoring the rumors with the nonchalance of the total professional, Brando arrived in England a few days before shooting began, just after completing his grueling stint in "Apocalypse Now." He had a cold and he looked tired, but he had trimmed over thirty pounds from his "Apocalypse" high and he seemed anxious to get started on "Superman."

The production office had spent weeks scouring the English countryside near the studio for a house suited to Brando and his party. But after a few nights at the estate, the actor requested a change, making it clear that "early nouveau riche" wasn't really his style. A more appropriate place was found, a forty-room restored Tudor mansion in Esher, and a phalanx of butlers, maids and gardeners were screened for efficiency, tact and discretion.

All this pampering seemed to put off some of the people on the production, particularly those who were aware of and admired Brando's reputation as a spokesman for the oppressed and as a man of simple tastes. The elaborate arrangements, however, had been part of a conscious effort by the production office, which, like all film production offices, held firmly to the credo that a comfortable, satisfied star is a star who gives a good performance . . . and *finishes on schedule!* (One evening, in fact, Brando had hot-water problems and for some reason ended up calling, of all people, the production accountant, Douglas Noakes. Noakes, anxious to help out, telephoned a plumber friend, and at ten o'clock at night the two men were climbing around the actor's house on ladders, trying to locate the rooftop water tank and the source of the problem.)

When the cameras finally turned over on the main stage that first day, most of the production personnel working on the film—along with the producers, Shepperton's administrators and a number of studio employees —were packed into the supposedly tightly guarded closed set, eager to grab at least a quick glimpse of the fabled actor.

As dictated by the call sheet, Brando's big black Daimler limousine pulled up to the studio gates promptly at 8:00 A.M.

His small entourage consisted of his long-time secretary, Alice Marchak, L. A. photographer Stefani Kong, and make-up artist Bill Rose.

Brando, wearing a pair of faded jeans and a T-shirt, looked somewhat drawn after his long trip, and he was still plagued by a bad head cold. But though the passage of time had added pounds to that famous physique, the clear blue eyes and chiseled profile were still unmistakably reminiscent of Napoleon, Mark Antony and Stanley Kowalski.

Scenes in a major picture are seldom shot in the sequence in which they appear in the final film; their order is determined, rather, by an actor's availability, studio scheduling, set construction, location, climate and the like. Accordingly, the first day's shooting on "Superman" required Brando as the long-dead Jor-El to sit perched on a stool—draped to the waist in black velvet, against an enormous black felt backing—and deliver a dramatic speech of instruction to his son, Kal-El (a.k.a. Superman), by means of an "education crystal."

Like any other film set, the stage was crammed with people and equipment—super Panavision cameras fitted with anamorphic lenses (designed to squeeze the image during photography and unsqueeze it during projection to produce an enlarged picture), assorted lights, recording gear, props, and an army of grips, gaffers and best boys (electrical or stage assistants). To make sure he would cover every possible angle on Brando, Dick Donner arranged to have, along with the three main unit cameras, three additional cameras, plus five possible back-ups, for a grand total of eleven!

But it wasn't the technical detail, however, that held everyone's attention that first day.

At about nine o'clock, Marlon Brando strolled casually onto the set, his shoulders already swathed in the black velvet. Smiling and nodding at both familiar and new faces, he shook hands with director Donner and the producers. Then, chatting with Alice Marchak, Stefani Kong and Bill Rose, he plunked himself down in a blue director's chair with his name stenciled on the back in white paint, As hairdresser Pat McDermott and several wardrobe assistants attended to him, he began to leaf through the morning papers.

When they actually started filming, most of us were surprised to see that Brando's lines had been carefully printed in marking pen or large posterboards that were positioned in front of the actor for each take. However, as Brando told us later, it's his firm belief that by memorizing lines, an actor loses his spontaneity and realism. He is convinced that by quickly sight-reading the cue cards while the cameras are turning, he can achieve— complete with pauses, hesitations and groping for words —more valid approximation of natural speaking. And after we had seen him work for a few days, most of us were in agreement with him.

Later in the morning, Christopher Reeve came on the set, eager to watch Brando work. The two men had met earlier in the day, when Marlon went to Chris's trailer to introduce himself. (Brando had also arranged to have a lavish basket of champagne and caviar from London's fashionable provisioners, Fortnum & Mason's, sent to Reeve's dressing room.)

It was the first time most of us had set eyes on our soon-to-be Superman, though a few Americans recognized him as Ben Harper from the old "Love of Life" TV soap. And even though Chris still had a lean and lanky look (in a matter of months, he would add over twenty pounds to his six-foot four-inch frame and two inches to his chest and biceps), we were all amazed at his striking resemblance to the comic-book Man of Steel: the same tall build, the same azure eyes, the same handsome chiseled features, the shy and slightly uneasy manner that was perfect for Clark Kent!

Chris strolled around the set during breaks in the filming, chatting and introducing himself to technicians and crew members. Like Brando, he was comfortably dressed: maroon crew-neck sweater, brown corduroy slacks and tan desert boots. Every now and then, Chris would walk to a corner of the cavernous stage and, oblivious to the activity all around him, do a few deep-knee bends and stretching exercises, designed to put him in shape for the grueling flying routines to come.

Yvonne Blake and her wardrobe assistant, Betty Adamson, hovered around the set with a hideous rubber doll figure of the baby Superman, the sight of which made Dick Donner cringe. "I remember Superman as a child," Yvonne informed me that morning, "and naturally, I had read the 'Superman' comics. So I started to prepare for the film by going to bed every night with a different comic book, just to get the feel of the thing and reacquaint myself with the character. However, when Richard took over the film, I was told that a lot of my ideas and concepts were *too much* like the comic; that, yes, we were working to preserve the legend, but that we had to go beyond the framework of the comics to make it much more realistic—you know, verisimilitude!"

The first day ran largely without a hitch, although as with all big productions, each set-up—positioning the cameras, lighting the stage, moving the sound equipment—seemed to take a great deal of time, even though it was far from an elaborate sequence.

Donner's reputation as a perfectionist, we all learned, is well earned. Someone sneezed loudly during a crucial take with Brando, and to break the tension the director shouted in his best booming baritone, "God bless you . . . and you're fired!"

● ● ●

Work began the next morning in Jor-El's laboratory, the first of the major sets to be utilized.

The set was a huge, fantastic, futuristic conglomeration of Lucite, styrofoam, Plexiglas, chrome and thousands of flashing lights (which raised the temperature on the floor to about 86 degrees!). Surrounding the entire center stage were massive white columns, illuminated by brilliant interior lights which reflected from hundreds of foil inserts.

"A motion picture has been described aptly as the world's biggest train set," art director John Barry told me. "But apart from the fun, I find the whole experience very educational. I started as an architect, and if I went back to that now, I'm sure I'd be a much better one for all my film work. I've been able to experiment, to explore—particularly thanks to big budgets—and I've learned much more about various forms and shapes and styles. And I know just what will work where in which materials. And if I don't like what I've done, I can throw it out. That's a privilege I don't think most architects have!

"Moviegoers are skillfully manipulated by filmmakers. It's our job to execute effortlessly the 'sleight of hand,' if you will. Images flash across the silver screen pretty quickly, and audiences shouldn't have time to dwell on what they see. They shouldn't say, 'Now wait a minute . . . did we see *all* of the car in that last shot or were the back wheels out of shot?' That's the sort of trick you have to get away with, especially with these complicated effects sequences.

"So many people have asked me how C-3PO, one of the robots in 'Star Wars,' worked, and I have to answer, 'Well, sometimes there was a man inside and sometimes he simply moved on tracks and wheels. The same was true for R2-D2. People seemed to want to believe that it was all so much more complex and sophisticated than it really was. They'd ask me, 'Did you operate him by computer? Did you design him with an integrated circuit?' and I'd have to smile and say, 'No, sometimes he was just pulled along on a piece of string!' And that's what it's all about with these movies: you have to cut a scene just where that proverbial 'piece of string' is about to show and spoil the fantasy. The director and the camera operator had the ability to cut the angle R2 was coming toward us at; the editor had the knack to cut the scene at the right point—there you have the perfect example.

"I like doing science fiction and fantasy films. You can let yourself go. I prefer designing surrealist things. I find it much easier, too, because you're free to choose. When you're in a jam, you can simply change the rules. Whereas if the script calls for you to duplicate the World Trade Center, it's got to *be* the World Trade Center; you can't say, 'Well, the plaster doesn't look right so let's paint the whole damn thing blue!' But if it's surrealist or fantasy, you can let your imagination take over. You can say, 'Right, this is all going to be sideways and that's going to be sticking out here and there's no gravity and good luck and so forth.'"

Barry sighed wistfully. "Of course, there are the limitations of time—and money. With a demanding film like 'Superman,' there's a high rate of turnover, an enormous number of sets that have to be ready for possible shooting the next day. And of course, the plans for every set have been endlessly complicated, because the principals don't just *walk* onto a set, they smash through walls or crash through doors—or *fly* in!

"The challenge is tremendous. Our star goes soaring through the air in blue woollies and red Wellington boots. And that's just for starters! We spent about a million pounds on the sets for 'Star Wars' and that was supposed to be a cheap movie. Just look what we're doing on *this* film!"

•   •   •

The mood on the set that whole first week was generally upbeat and exciting. We were elated to be on a film like "Superman" with a star like Brando, and we enjoyed getting acclimated to one another, learning each other's particular style and method of getting things done.

I have for some time believed that making a motion picture is like a major military operation, and that opinion was confirmed by this production, with scores of assistants running around relaying messages through crackling walkie-talkies. (Pierre, whose first language is French—noun before adjective—referred to them as "talkie-walkies.")

•   •   •

A few days into the shooting, Brando's cold got the best of him and he telephoned Dick Donner to say that he just couldn't make it to the studio. A tense but understanding Donner told the star to stay home and take it easy, and a grim-looking Pierre Spengler paced the set during the test shots with the dummy baby which were scheduled in Brando's absence. But at the end of his stint on the film, a good-natured Marlon gave the producers an extra day of shooting beyond his contractual obligation—no mean gift at his astronomical salary. (One of the favorite pastimes of the crew in those early days was to figure out, between setups, a breakdown of Brando's fee for the picture. It worked out to something like $245,000 per nine-hour day or roughly $27,000 per hour, $450 per minute, or approximately $8 a second. At that rate, production assistant Michael Green calculated, Marlon could have ordered a spanking new Rolls-Royce from Jack Barclay's in London and damn near had it paid for before the driver made it to Shepperton!)

•   •   •

To shoot some of the scenes of the destruction of Krypton and Jor-El's laboratory, the fabulous set on "A" stage had to be destroyed in several phases and "dressed" accordingly.

The setup took a great deal of time and preparation, with Geoff Unsworth bringing in additional lighting equipment, much of it fitted with red filters to achieve the proper fiery effect, and set dresser Peter Howitt and an army of Georgie Ball's prop men scattering tons of debris and foam-rubber rubble.

As soon as Marlon and Susannah York arrived on the stage, Betty Adamson and her wardrobe assistants began applying extra strips of material to their phantasmagoric costumes, designed in reflecting "front projection" paper. A silvery substance made up of thousands of light-sensitive beads—used primarily for front and back film projection in special-effects sequences—the "FP" paper, which cost hundreds of dollars per short roll, created an eerie, glowing aura when the lights were directed onto the two stars. Because of the special reflecting quality of the "FP" material, anyone handling the delicate paper had to use white cotton gloves so as not to destroy the surface with grubby fingerprints.

With each shot on this set, Unsworth and his gaffer (chief electrician) Johnny Tythe added more overhead high-intensity spots wrapped in red cellophane, creating a burning, volcanic glow on the disintegrating laboratory.

The sequence involved the violent eruptions which shatter Jor-El's lab just prior to the departure of the starship that will carry the baby Kal-El to Earth and safety. After each take (Elaine Schreyech carefully recording which piece of rubble was where), John Barry and his assistants would coordinate the elaborate state of disarray, with Colin Chivers and the mechanical-effects people rigging up the breakaways.

During the first take, Brando and York huddled amidst crashing debris—mainly blackened chunks of styrofoam, silver "glitter," and jagged pieces of reflective material.

Just before Dick yelled "Cut!" Marlon slipped and fell in a puddle of water created by the dripping fog and steam machines that had been employed to give the entire set a smoldering quality. Brando picked himself up, with a bit of help from Susannah, as the director and his assistants ran over to make sure he was all right. The wardrobe assistants rushed to make on-the-spot repairs to his ethereal Kryptonian costume.

On the second take, Donner had the two stars run across the set, dodging the debris being dropped from huge sliding panels above the stage at precisely the right moment. The tension and excitement built, the lights in the pulsing white columns flickered and dimmed, and then with a deafening roar the floor collapsed directly in front of the fleeing actors, forming a gaping cavern. As the horrified Jor-El and Lara froze in their tracks, an exhausted Donner shouted "Cut!" and the crew, almost as a single body, breathed a sigh of relief.

At the end of that first week—all days of dreary, damp, drizzly weather—"A" stage looked as if it had received a direct bomb hit. And to add to the sense of devastation, extra fog machines were brought in, filling the set with foul-smelling, acrid smoke.

By then Terence Stamp had arrived at Shepperton to begin his part as the malevolent General Zod—nemesis of Jor-El, and ultimately arch-foe of Superman—who is banished, along with the man-hating Ursa and the bestial Non, to the Phantom Zone by Jor-El and the August Council of Elders of Krypton.

•　　•　　•

One afternoon, I left the studio early and joined our film documentary crew at the Grosvenor House Hotel gym in the fashionable Mayfair section of London to watch Chris Reeve in one of his rigorous daily workouts.

The sweaty, noisy gym was a sharp contrast to the lobby of this stately bastion of old-world elegance, crowded now with German, French, Japanese and American tourists.

Chris's routine involved a series of limbering-up exercises, weightlifting, "pumping iron," and much grunting, panting and sweating. Every now and then, he would pause, flushed, to chat with the documentary cameramen and Brando's photographer, Stefani Kong, also there to record the regimen.

The scene was bizarre, with lighting and sound men working around all the equipment, and surprised hotel guests, who had wandered in to use the facilities and found a film unit in the small orange-and-brown-carpeted gym.

"We all want Superman to be real," Chris told me during a brief test period. "I guess I was something of a stringbean. But the producers and the director saw the potential—after all, I am six feet four and I started at a hundred eighty-nine pounds. After just a few weeks of these tough hour-and-a-half workouts—plus a very demanding *eating* schedule!—I'm already up to two hundred two pounds."

• • •

At the beginning of Brando's second week, filming shifted to another of Barry's startlingly futuristic sets.

This was the Council Chamber, where an impassioned Jor-El attempts to convince his doubting peers (among others, Maria Schell, Trevor Howard and Harry Andrews) that the planet Krypton is doomed.

The entire stage was an awesome mixture of polyethylene tubing, Lucite and plastics. The intense arc lights brought the temperature up to 95 degrees after a few hours, which made it almost unbearable for the principals, all wearing heavy tunics of reflective "FP" material. Brando's make-up artist had to dab the actor's sweat-soaked brow with tissue continually between takes, while Pat McDermott combed back stray locks of the carefully arranged snow-white wig—except, of course, the single curl purposely draped across Brando's forehead, Superman-style.

At the center of the set was a revolving Lucite disk, lit from beneath the stage. Above this, serving as sort of a "witness stand" in the Council Chambers, were two stainless steel rings, counterbalanced and spinning in opposite directions. "Floating" between the two rings was a configuration of clear and smoked Lucite.

The scene called for Vond-Ah (Maria Schell) to challenge Jor-El's theory that Krypton is going to explode. Jor-El was to reply with a powerful speech claiming that beyond a shadow of a doubt Krypton was doomed. Unfortunately, Trevor Howard kept missing his cue and stepping on Marlon's lines. But a patient Brando at last got through his speech. Then, just as he delivered his lines about the fast-approaching eruption of the planet, a glass reflector shield on one of the cameras burst from the intense heat, shattering into a million shards. After making sure that no one was hurt, Dick Donner laughingly assured us that it was an *omen* that "Superman" was going to be . . . a smash!

●　　●　　●

The producers were still embroiled in casting problems, the most crucial of which was finding the right Lois Lane. (At lunch one day, Chris told of how he had been reduced to speechlessness when Susan Blakely, fresh from her screen test for the part, sat down to chat with him, removed her chewing gum, and stuck it to the bottom of one of his shoes.) Ilya Salkind and Pierre Spengler, along with Donner, spent most of the four-day Easter shooting break trying to fill the female lead.

After the brief holiday, Sarah Douglas and big Jack O'Halloran arrived to join Terry Stamp in their roles as the three super-villains of "Superman" I and II—since the Salkinds had kept to their plan of filming two pictures simultaneously, adding to the complexity of the operation.

Yvonne Blake's costuming for the three villains was a tour de force of imaginative evil. The trio was severely outfitted in shiny black jumpsuits, trimmed in glowing deep maroon vinyl, and matching hip-high boots. (Jack's boots had five-inch platforms, so that he just about reached seven feet!) All of them had dead-white base make-up, with their eyes and cheeks shadowed in black. Sarah's costume had side vents, and her hairdo was a close-cropped "butch" style—actually a wig; her real hair is almost waist-length—and as a final accent, Stuart Freeborn gave her jet-black lipstick and nail polish.

• • •

One afternoon, with much activity on the floor, I decided to climb one of the lighting department's ladders and survey the entire chaotic panorama from the scaffolding above the stage. And this particular day provided me with a scene of marvelous counter-point.

Off in one of the darker corners of this enormous set on this super-budget production—out of the proximity of Marlon Brando and the hundreds of extras, camera crews, costume designers and assorted technicians—stood little Alex Salkind, the master of it all, pensively smoking a cigarette, stroking his wavy mane of luxuriant silver hair and toying with the Legion d' Honneur rosette in his lapel, silently soaking up everything with his piercing blue eyes.

• • •

Christopher Reeve's first day of shooting on the picture involved his only direct, face-to-face scene with Brando.

Reeve arrived early on "G" stage to rehearse the scene (from "Superman II") which called for him, as a powerless Clark Kent, to travel to Superman's secret Fortress of Solitude, hidden away deep in the frozen Arctic. Bruised and battered from a scuffle with street thugs, torn between the demands of his true identity as the Man of Steel—champion of "truth, justice and the American way"—and his love for Lois Lane (who now knows Clark's *real* identity), Kal-El confronts the enduring spirit of his father Jor-El with his painful dilemma.

* * *

Brando was in a particularly upbeat mood right through the final days of his stint on "Superman," despite the often complicated and slow-moving "process" shots (involving special projection) his scenes called for.

The set for the indictment of the three super-villains was a large, black, circular, elevated platform. In the center of this platform was another rotating double-ringed device like the witness stand in the Council Chamber, but much larger. This would serve as the temporary "cell" in which Zod, Ursa and Non would await their sentences.

Behind the platform was a mammoth semicircular black backdrop onto which the looming bluish faces of the Council members were projected. This was accomplished by a series of small windowlike openings at the base of the backdrop, through which the previously filmed images were projected onto large mirrors carefully positioned around the base of the stage. The mirrors were angled upward to enlarge the images which "materialized" on the backdrop-screen. To heighten the ghostly effect and the mood of impending doom, the smoke machines were again brought in and placed around the periphery of the huge stage, with large fans positioned in front of them to distribute the smoke and create a dense haze.

Because of the difficulties of coordination and timing involved with process work, filming the foreground action of Brando and the villains against the projected background images took long, tedious hours, with many retakes. I was amazed at everyone's powers of concentration, finding myself disconcerted even by the slight edge-of-frame flicker from the projected images (not visible, of course, in the final print) when they first appeared on the backdrop.

I was more rattled, however, by the bold letter "S" emblazoned on Brando's black velvet caftan. As I understood it, that was the emblem of Superman himself, *not* his family name! In the midst of all this intricate filming, I cornered the director to point out the seeming gaffe. Not to worry, I was told. In fact, retaining this modified element of Puzo's treatment had been a joint decision by Donner himself and scriptwriter Mankiewicz, to further establish both the real and symbolic bond between father and son.

During the two days required to shoot this scene, Marlon's playfulness between takes became more pronounced. If he wasn't standing around, twirling his Staff of Judgement and Authority and joking with Dick and the crew, then he was sneaking up alongside Sarah Douglas and slipping his hand into one of the vents of her costume. The crew, in turn, were becoming equally good-humored with the star, referring to him affectionately as "Marvin Rando."

Brando's last day on the picture involved a particularly tedious and slow-going series of "pick-ups" (extra scenes or retakes) and matte shots. Basically, a matte shot consists of photographically blending painted material with live action. A portion of what is actually being filmed by the cameras is blocked (matted) out so that the artwork can be carefully fitted in later.

Sitting around between takes, draped in black velvet against the familiar black backdrop, Marlon bantered with Donner, asking him how, since everything was running so slowly today, he had managed the frantic sequence of a pack of wild baboons attacking Lee Remick's car in a particularly frightening scene in "The Omen"?

"Simple," the director said, deadpan. "I just yelled 'ACTION!'"

After the "wrap" at 5:30, everyone was invited over to "D" stage for the party Alex, Ilya and Pierre had arranged in Marlon's honor. Brando made the rounds, chatting with and thanking just about every crew member and autographing dozens of photographs. (A couple of pranksters on the set had taken the director's chair, with RICHARD DONNER boldly lettered on the back, and blacked out a few strategic letters with gaffer tape, so that the chair now read HARD ON, much to Donner's amusement.)

• • •

A few days before he finished his "Superman" stint, Brando granted me a forty-five-minute interview, one of the few he had permitted in recent years. The three-quarters of an hour I spent with him on the set revealed to me a complex man of considerable strength, conspicuous talent, wide-ranging intelligence and great conviction. He answered all my questions directly and cheerfully.

What did he think about playing the father of one of America's greatest legendary heroes?

"I think I'll make a lot of money," Brando grinned. "To tell the truth, I don't really remember Superman when I was a kid. Of course, everyone knows Superman, so the film has a good chance of being successful. But then, I don't know. I think if you're twenty feet away from a donkey and you've got six cabbages, you don't know whether or not you are ever going to get the donkey with the cabbages . . . all you've got is a good chance."

Had Brando read any of the conflicting stories about his salary, his health, his latest romance or his future plans in the *Evening Standard* or any of the other London papers?

"I never met with anyone from the *Evening Standard*. I guess they feel free to just make things up. They should be held accountable—a line has to be drawn somewhere. But then, that's like asking hookers to draw their own lines. And there are five-hundred-dollar hookers, or twenty-five-dollar hookers. There are all kinds of lines. . . .

"I've enjoyed working in England very much, though. I've enjoyed the people—they're courteous, they have a sense of . . . of style . . . and of manner that's based on hundreds of years of civilization. Living in the culture we have in America, we're in a state of perpetual change. Our culture is change *based on change*. Everything has to be new, every two minutes, so that we have no sense of tradition, no roots. That's one of the reasons why Americans—white Americans—were so impressed by the television production 'Roots.' I think everybody in America yearns to have some kind of roots. The native American Indians *do* have roots, they *do* have a sense of heritage, because after all, *they* were the first Americans.

"The government of the United States claims to be concerned about human rights, about upholding personal freedoms. I think it seems a mark of gross hypocrisy for the U.S. government to say to the world, 'We're interested in your welfare, your freedoms, your political redemption,' when we ignore the injustices to the American Indians committed by our own country. After the last war, we were willing to assist Germany, we were willing to help Japan . . . we seem willing to aid North Vietnam, for whatever reasons . . . all without great sacrifices on our part. So it seems a puzzle that we will *not* do it for the Indians. Just think how our prestige in the world would increase if we did do something to rectify that."

Because of his fame, hadn't Brando been able to open doors and make himself heard in his dedicated campaign of support for the American Indians?

"Well, let me give you one example." Brando sighed. I was criticized roundly when I refused the Academy

Award, letting an Indian speak for me. I honestly felt that an Indian, for the first time in America, should have the right to address the sixty or eighty million people who watch the Awards show. I was criticized for not coming myself. So this past year, after the Academy had asked for permission to run clips from some of my films, I wrote back and said yes, I would be happy to say O.K. if they would allow me to come before them, on the program, to express my views, to rebut the criticism resulting from my refusal to accept the Award. And they replied curtly that the Academy Awards 'is not a political platform.'"

What would Brando be doing next?

"I'm already involved in a series of thirteen one-hour films about the native American Indians—sort of an Indian 'Roots'—that will take up most of my time. It is being financed privately, through a foundation, and will be nonprofit. I will not receive any recompense for it. Money earned will go to the Indian people themselves. I'd like to use my fame, my 'notoriety,' for the purpose of disseminating information about the environment. And that certainly includes the political environment as well."

That was fine for this one project, I said. As a rule, though, didn't the world depend on profit and revolve around the dollar?

"I think it does. But it seems to me that we're all living under the illusion that the making of money is going to increase our happiness in direct proportion. Rich people jump out the window at the same rate poor people do."

Brando had, in fact, been quoted in the press as saying that all of his astronomical "Superman" salary would be put into his current film project about the Indians. I managed to steer him back to "Superman."

"Superman is a heroic symbol to children," he said. "*All* children—because they're small and because they feel uncomfortable and inferior to adults—have fantasies.

—76—

They enjoy themes which they can be a part of, where they can be big. They enjoy seeing themselves as Superman. So it will be a big release for them to go and see this film. And most of their parents will go too, because so many of the parents feel helpless in the face of taxes, laws, chaos, crime—the 'distress of life.' They feel helpless to do anything, so it's good for them. And, naturally, it's enjoyable. There are times you just want some kind of popcorn and happiness. We all have to find a way to unwind. All this getting and spending—it gets to us."

At that point, we noticed our executive producer walking across the stage toward us, elegantly attired and replete with threaded gold chains.

"Hi ya, Ilya," Brando called. Then smiling broadly, he confided to me, "*This* is the hard part."

5
The not-so-lovely month
of May

Confidential memo from Pierre Spengler to Dick Donner:
"General Comment: We have never really gone into the
mechanics of Superman flying. We know he can fly because he is from Krypton, but we still do not know what
mechanically makes him fly."

Producer Spengler could hardly have realized, dashing
off this casual comment about the script in late April,
how horrendously prophetic his words were. Because
getting Superman to fly—and making it look thoroughly
believable on the screen—presented the beleaguered
Donner and his experienced crew with seemingly insur-
mountable problems that more than once almost shut
down the entire production.

The director's demand for perfection, along with un-
realistic schedules, lack of time, inadequate testing, concepts that worked better in theory than in practice—all
this contributed to the agonizing difficulties that plagued
Superman's "flight crew" in the months ahead. The flying problem contributed to the first perceptible tensions
between the director and the producers, which began
to manifest themselves in May.

•   •   •

After Brando's departure from the film, the whole production slipped into a discernible depression.

The let-down feeling continued through the last few days of April, during which Donner and Tom Mankiewicz—who had been at Shepperton, furiously typing out script revisions—flew off for quick casting sessions in L.A. and then a recon of locations in Canada. The fact that during this time the main unit shot little more than tests and pick-up shots did nothing to lift the general malaise.

To liven things up a bit, our amiable runner, Paul Storey, let us know that Elton John was presently rehearsing on one of the special recording sound stages for a concert in London. Between takes, Paul would take me and a few of the camera boys or prop department people up to a darkened, glass-enclosed listening booth high above the stage to enjoy our own private concert by the fabled glitter-rock star.

When Donner returned to England, his crew was ready to prepare for the first of what would turn out to be hundreds of flying shots with Christopher Reeve. In the long months of planning and pre-production and all through the extended shooting, an amazing variety of flying techniques was tested, modified, tossed out . . . with a few eventually ending up in the final print. Sometimes Wally Veevers and Denys Coop, director of photography of the flying unit, would use tried-and-true methods incorporating front projection, sometimes they'd go for procedures never before attempted, sometimes an amalgamation of both. In the course of the film, Veevers and the other specialists talked about, tested, and finally used everything from flying harnesses, hydraulic armatures, Chapman cranes, and animated models to depressurized weightless chambers, underwater photography, and sky diving. Throughout it all, a stoic Christopher Reeve remained firm about doing most of his own stunt work. And by the time the picture wrapped, neither Chris nor anyone else would deny that the flying had been the single most difficult aspect of the filming of "Superman."

"The advances in film technology over the past few years have been staggering," Dick Donner told me, "and the special effects in each major production seem to take the art one step further. Audiences have become very sophisticated, very tough. They won't accept mediocrity . . . remember those awful horror films of the fifties? When Superman streaks across the screen, it's gotta look a helluva lot better than Mary Martin dangling from a few wires in 'Peter Pan'!"

The director, accompanied by Pierre Spengler and North American locations manager Tim Burrill, even went to the new National Air and Space Museum in Washington, D.C. in his effort to perfect the flying techniques. At the museum, the three men saw the much-acclaimed 45-minute documentary "To Fly," filmed on 70-millimeter stock and projected on a screen five stories high, giving the audience an edge-of-the-seat view of flight. Though Donner was impressed, the added cost of shooting "Superman" in 70mm would have skyrocketed the budget beyond all reason and would have necessitated replacing existing projection equipment in most movie theaters. (However, in fact, some 70mm prints *will* be specially prepared.)

With Chris back from a quick trip to the States, complete with a head cold and croup, Donner was ready to shoot tests for the initial flying sequences. Somehow, the entire atmosphere of the rehearsal was unavoidably, slightly comic. Chris had just finished telling us, quite seriously, about his wariness of the press's attitude toward the "Superman" film, and of his own absolute insistence on maintaining a strict separation between Chris Reeve the man and his persona as Superman. Seeing him in his tan slacks, striped jersey and sneakers, strapped into a leather flying rig, coughing and sneezing, I found it a little hard to believe that Chris would be able to achieve that aim. Anyway, Donner and everyone else were sure of one thing—the flying had a long way to go.

While construction of the massive interiors of the Fortress of Solitude continued on "H" stage, the main unit finished up the sequences of the destruction of Krypton. It all looked great, with an army of extras crashing through acres of Plexiglas, Lucite and styrofoam. Unfortunately, during one of the takes, a stunt man was slightly injured when one of the crystal stalagmites failed to disappear on cue, so the scene had to be reshot.

It was at this time that Dick and Tom Mankiewicz had Margot Kidder brought over for the screen test with Chris that got her the part of Lois Lane. Obviously still suffering from severe jet-lag, Margot nonetheless sauntered jauntily into the Shepperton commissary in tight Levis, pigtails and ten-gallon hat. Arriving with her was eighteen-year-old Californian Jeff East, who would play the young Clark Kent.

The Canadian-born Kidder, who had starred in "The Great Waldo Pepper" opposite Robert Redford and in "The Reincarnation of Peter Proud," was high on Donner's list of potential Loises. Because of the suddenness of her arrival, Margot showed up for her test with Chris wearing a hastily chosen and unflattering dress. And to the horror of assistant director Steve Lanning, planted directly on top of her carefully coiffed, if inappropriate, wig was the ten-gallon hat! However, on viewing the rushes of her test, Donner and the producers agreed that her performance had a certain spark and vitality. Also strong was her interaction with Chris. More importantly, as Donner explained to Ilya and Pierre, Margot seemed to convey the general American concept of Lois Lane—pretty, pert and perky, intelligent and ambitious without being pushy. After she was told that she had the part, Margot ran off to Beauchamp Place to buy all that silk underwear.

Now that the decision to cast Margot had been made,

Dick Donner had the unenviable task of calling another actress, Leslie Ann Warren, who had been at the top of his personal list. I happened to be in his office at the time, trying to complete an interview with him, and so was able to hear his end of the phone call. Donner's approach to Warren was intimate, understanding and genuinely regretful; it was clear that the director was experiencing personal anguish. But as soon as he put down the phone, Donner perked up and dived back into "Superman."

As soon as construction on "H" stage was completed, Dick was ready for the flying rehearsals to begin in earnest. "H" stage at Shepperton is a huge, cavernous building on a far corner of the back lot of the studio. John Barry's imaginative set for the interior of the Fortress of Solitude was designed to resemble a gigantic crystalline cavern, formed when young Clark Kent hurls into the Arctic sea the crystal Jor-El had carefully placed in the starship that carried his young son to Earth. The entire set—plywood, styrofoam, plastic, polyethylene tubing and mirrored glass—had been sprinkled with reflective glitter and dusted with styrofoam "snow" from the North Pole exterior. When it was fogged over with dry ice and lit by Geoff Unsworth in bright white light, along with hazy tones of blue and green, the whole stage took on an ethereal, otherworldly quality that was remarkably impressive.

These flying shots marked Chris's first appearance in the world-renowned Superman costume. The afternoon rehearsals were to start, he showed up in the studio restaurant after several hours' preparation, wearing a white terrycloth dressing robe and several layers of Stuart Freeborn's carefully applied make-up. With the deepened flesh tones and jet-black, perfectly styled Superman hairdo, complete with curled forelock—Chris's hair had to be rinsed periodically with a black dye, his own natural color being sandy brown, and Pat McDermott had also ordered several wigs—he looked every inch the Man of Steel. And when he removed his robe and stood revealed in the red boots, billowing red cape and bright blue leotard with the familiar "S" emblazoned boldly on the chest, Reeve was awe inspiring.

As much as he looked the part, however, Chris made it clear when he talked to me later on the set that the film Superman would have to have greater depth of character than the comic-book figure.

"A hero should *not know* he's a hero—otherwise he becomes pretentious and boring. Somebody put it very well when he said. 'You can't *play* the king; the people around you play to you being king.

"It's important to humanize Superman. He walks through walls and can hold up the Golden Gate Bridge with his hands and so forth. So if on top of all that he said to himself, 'My God, am *I* good!' then you'd have a real prig, a boring piece of cardboard. So what I'm trying to do is to go way under. If the script calls for incredible feats, all I have to do is . . . just simply do them. What makes Superman a hero is not that he has power, but that he has the wisdom and the maturity to use the power wisely. From an acting point of view, that's how I approach the part.

"Another human element I perceive is that he's not always secure—he doesn't always have all the answers.

"Staying with the theme of making him more human, take the scene we'll do on Lois's balcony, when Superman comes flying in. The script had it that he was really there only to impress her—that's what I got from the first script—that he's sort of showing off. Now *I* think it's quite the other way around; he's there because he's got a crush on her. Superman has already lost his heart; he just saw Lois Lane for the first time and went nuts. Because that's part of the American ideal, too—love at first sight. You know, it's marrying your teenage sweetheart. And then, he's modest enough and relaxed enough not to have to hijack her—so that when he comes in as Superman, I want the audience to see that he's there just because he wants to spend time with the girl he likes. And if the problem is, can he let her know who he is? then that's painfully boring too. Where's the conflict? Where's the doubt? Where are the problems? Some people seem to think that Superman is totally invincible—both physically and emotionally—but he's *not*. Part of being human is having doubt and conflict and worry and struggle. And though he *is* from Krypton, all those characteristics need to be in our Superman. That's why I put a tension between Superman and Clark Kent. There are elements of each character in the other . . . sometimes Superman would like to be Clark Kent, just a normal person with normal responsibilities. Clark Kent would certainly like to reveal himself as Superman so that Lois Lane would care for him more; there's a tension of identity going on there. Another thing . . . it's important that Superman adopts a very good disguise. That's why I'll go to considerable lengths to try to make the *character* a good disguise. Up till now, he's been played with a pair of glasses and no other behavioral change. But I feel it must be really fundamental, because otherwise Lois Lane's an idiot! For thirty years, in the comic, she's never figured out that Clark and Superman are the same person. Now, either she's a dodo or he's very good at his disguise, and I've decided that he's very good at his disguise.

"For me, that extends the range of what he has and what his father told him to do. When I come flying onto the balcony—if you've got a man who comes flying in over Brooklyn and around the World Trade Center and ends up on the balcony, then naturally he should just go 'Hi!', you know, as if he just came from the street corner. Because if he comes flying in and then poses and thinks he looks magnificent—please, who needs it?—you'd send him away."

Before a.d.'s Roy Button and Steve Lanning led Chris off to David Tomblin so that he could be strapped into his specially designed leather flying harness, he summed up, grinning, "I want Superman to be somebody that, you know, you can invite home for dinner . . . someone you could introduce your parents to."

After day-time shooting, most of the set on "H" stage had to be dismantled (hence John Barry's movable crystal "glaciers") to make room for the evening flying tests, a fact which compounded the problems of the director, Chris, the stunt team and the crew.

Reeve's great difficulty, even after months of practice, appeared to be in keeping his limbs ramrod-straight so that his body weight would be evenly distributed, a muscle-straining task when one is suspended in midair. This was essential to prevent him from traveling crookedly, which the flying unit called "crabbing." With a nervous, chain-smoking Dick Conner pacing back and forth on one of the "glaciers" between each setup, Chris, tightly belted into his flying gear (by the end of the film, he had gone from big black-and-blue marks to calluses), would wait patiently while Colin Chilvers and the effects department struggled with the finishing touches required for each particular shot.

•   •   •

With the growing problems of the flying sequences, and new hitches cropping up daily, the producers anxiously noted that in mid-May the film was already more than a week behind schedule. And they were losing more ground every day.

A worried-looking Pierre Spengler, chewing distractedly on a cigarette holder jammed in the corner of his mouth, his thin, bearded face increasingly drawn, spent hours at his desk talking by phone to Alex or bent over a tiny pocket calculator.

Rumors of growing tension between Donner and the producers gave the crew something to gossip about and broke the temporary tedium on the set. So, too, did the steady stream of visitors (all with the apparent blessing of either the producers or Donner, despite the "closed set" status of the film).

One of the more memorable visits was that of a group of twenty-five wounded Israeli veterans. The men and women, all survivors of Middle East conflicts from 1948 through the Yom Kippur War of 1973, were enthusiastic about touring the studio and amazingly high-spirited, despite the fact that many of them were missing limbs or were severely disfigured. I found it particularly poignant when one young paratrooper, joking with a receptive Chris Reeve, laughingly informed us through an interpreter that he was available if the producers needed "a slightly damaged Superman!"

Things picked up, too, with the presence of Valerie Perrine and Gene Hackman. Bubbling, chatty and uninhibited ("earthy" is a mild description), Perrine arrived with a small group of friends and immediately made the rounds and met most of the key people on the production. In the restaurant her first day, she organized a little "get-to-know-you" lunch with Donner, Tom Mankiewicz, Chris and Jeff East.

While there was equal interest and excitement about Hackman, we had been warned by crew members who'd worked with him before that he was a "very private person." Certainly little was seen of him—through no fault of his own, though—during his first days at the studio while he submitted to costume and wig fittings necessitated by the revised script—to the tune of $52,000 a day in overage!

With two more major stars on the lot and stories—most of them erroneous—being leaked to the press about the "Superman" special effects, the producers decided to clamp an even tighter lid on the entire production. So Ilya Salkind, along with Gordon Arnell, visiting Warner Brothers' ad-pub VP Andy Fogelson and other publicity executives, issued the first of many security edicts, dated May 13, 1977: "After a series of discussions with Warner Brothers, who will distribute 'Superman' in many major territories, it has been decided to institute a completely new approach to the film's promotion which we expect to create an even greater interest than at present.

"In the near future we shall be sending you all a detailed letter explaining the precise procedures we should like to be taken in dealing with anyone outside the immediate film unit.

"As a general rule we should like to keep our activities TOP SECRET.

"We are doing things seldom, if ever, attempted on film before and need everybody's cooperation in preparing to present 'Superman' to the world at exactly the right moment and as a MAJOR EVENT worthy of your efforts."

The CIA and Interpol could probably have taken a few cues from the "Superman" production office, because two months later, *Time* magazine was calling the film "the most supersecret, superpublicized"—a kind of contradiction in terms, I thought—movie ever to be shot.

●　　●　　●

By the end of May, the shooting was almost a full two weeks behind schedule—and along with production and casting problems, the producers had the pressure of preparing for the annual Cannes Film Festival. In years past, the Salkinds had been a dominant presence at the Festival, and 1977—the year of "Superman's" production start—wasn't likely to see a change in that familiar pattern. (Young Salkind and Spengler considered hiring an executive jet to shuttle them between their London base and the South of France each weekend of the Festival!)

At this time, final plans were being made to shift everything to Pinewood Studios, a move necessitated by the steadily expanding size of the production as well as what was then perceived as the advantage of being based at a fully staffed full-service studio.

So with construction work on the *Daily Planet* offices already begun on "E" stage at Pinewood, Donner moved to wrap up main-unit shooting at Shepperton as quickly as possible. The flying unit would, in fact, stay behind for several weeks' more work on the interior of the Fortress—and thus, for a while, "Superman" spanned two studios. (By the end of production, it would involve *three.*)

Despite the growing tension over the delays, filming during those last few days at Shepperton generally progressed smoothly. (To gain extra time and hold down the spiraling costs, it was decided that the location work on "Superman II" set for Washington, D.C., would be shelved indefinitely. Though the producers optimistically claimed that the shooting would be rescheduled "at a later date," the decision raised the first of many serious doubts about preserving the integrity of the multimillion dollar film project.) Donner and Hackman were often cutting up between takes; sometimes during setups, giant Jack O'Halloran and Margot Kidder would tap dance or run through a medley of songs from "West Side Story" while perched precariously atop one of the tiered styrofoam crystal "glaciers." The massive set itself made these antics incongruous enough, and the actors' outfits added memorably to the effect, with Gene looking like a Chase Manhattan banker in his pinstripe suit and gold watch chain, Jack in his pseudo-S-and-M gear and Margot in "girl Friday" matching jacket and skirt. The skylarking was risky business, as demonstrated when O'Halloran's stunt double, Jack Cooper, went crashing through the top of a glacier which hadn't been properly reinforced, luckily escaping with only minor cuts and bruises.

During one break between shots, I tried to finish up an informal interview with Margot as she rushed about her dressing room in various states of undress—from near to total—eager to get to Heathrow Airport to pick up her arriving baby daughter Maggie. "Look, don't mind me," Margot said unabashedly as she threw everything together and raced out the door. "I was an early hippie, so I'm not into all this modesty shit!"

• • •

At this point in the production, people were getting to know one another—working together, socializing off the set in the evening hours.

Naturally, being based in England with a primarily British crew meant that the majority of the technicians and the production office personnel headed for home when shooting wrapped each day. Dick Donner would usually race back to London in his black vintage Rolls-Royce convertible, preferring a quiet evening at his Chelsea flat so that he could be up and alert for his 6:30 morning call. Margot was busy setting up a home-away-from-home for herself and her daughter. Gene Hackman's off-camera activities were a mystery to most of the members of the production. Only hyperactive Valerie Perrine kept up a nonstop social schedule, making the circuit of Mr. Chow's, Trader Vic's and every "in" club and disco.

Putting his work before everything else, Chris Reeve did very little fraternizing with anyone from the "Superman" company, preferring, like Donner, to make it an early night. Still, the London press and international wire services were full of stories and photographs of Reeve squiring an assortment of attractive young women to important parties, openings, and Tramp's or other trendy London boîtes.

"I'm not here to win a popularity contest," Reeve told me. "I'm not here to have fun. I'm here to put something on the screen that's going to entertain people later. I mean, you go to a party on Friday and by Monday no one remembers you were there. But they'll *always* remember what you put on the screen—good or bad. And I have a responsibility to see that it's good.

"That's why I'm willing to make the sacrifices that I do . . . that's why I'm antisocial to the extent that I am. I come home every day from work, sometimes in agony because I feel that a scene wasn't one hundred percent. I keep thinking, 'It's all right, they'll fix it with music or they'll play it on Brando or Hackman and he'll save me on that scene.' Sometimes I really think that way. I guess I'm driven. So that's why when I'm walking around the set, I can't take visitors, I can't take screwing around, I can't take lateness. I go nuts, because I'm so rigidly focused into the work."

Then *what* did Reeve do for "fun" off-camera?

"A lot." He smiled, his face lighting up. "You see, when I work, I do nothing but work and when I play, I do nothing but play. Music is very important to me— I've played the piano for about ten years. Flying—the kind in planes!—is my other interest. I fly both planes and gliders. I'm also an avid sailor, skier, tennis player— those are basically my main vices."

•   •   •

With May almost over, the weather improving, and relations between Donner and the producers deteriorating daily, the "Superman" production packed up for the move to a new home base.

6

Supercannes

Pinewood Studios, a sprawling complex spread out over one hundred idyllic acres near the village of Iver in tranquil Buckinghamshire, is the most complete—and comfortable—"full service" film studio in England and quite probably the best in Europe. Certainly it was one of the few studios outside the United States able to accommodate a production on the scale of "Superman."

Dating back to the mid-thirties heyday of motion pictures, Pinewood is a far cry from California's Universal City or the Burbank Studios. Built around a stately ivy-covered rural manor house, a Victorian mansion called Heatherden Hall, it has, over the years, successfully blended modern-day filmmaking with an aura of old-world grace and slightly faded elegance.

The entrance to the administration building, where the producers' offices were located, is framed by an enormous, intricately carved, solid oak Elizabethan fireplace, the date 1561 chiseled across the top timber.

Pinewood is as unlike a "factory" studio as it can be without threatening efficiency of operation. And whatever the studio may lack in the way of latest equipment or facilities, it more than makes up for in excellent working conditions and top-flight personnel.

The main office complex overlooks beautifully manicured gardens that resemble a mini-Versailles, and have been used for shooting many scenes. To the left and slightly behind the administration building are the restaurant and pub—there is also a decidedly dismal canteen—which open out onto the lovely tree-lined pathways. (On the rare warm sunny day, most people at Pinewood take time out to sit under a shade tree and enjoy a pint of ale.) The cavernous restaurant, which once was the ballroom of Heatherden Hall, is paneled in polished wood from the old Cunard liner *Mauretania,* bought as scrap forty-odd years ago for the bargain price of 78 pounds sterling. Of course, anyone wanting a change from the studio environment can bicycle the short distance to the nearby pubs—The Black Horse, The Traveller's Friend, The Gurkha, The Stag—which dot the surrounding countryside.

More to the point for filmmakers, Pinewood offers an enormous back lot, a huge tank (where movies such as "A Night to Remember" were photographed), and fifteen stages, including the towering "007 Stage," built for Cubby Broccoli's most recent Bond epic—at 374' by 160' by 53' reputedly the largest stage in the world.

*   *   *

With everyone shuttling back and forth between Shepperton and Pinewood in the final stages of the move, Mario Puzo arrived for a brief visit. The creator of The Godfather, genial and unpretentious, joked and chatted with a number of us, took a brief tour of the set with Dick and several key crew members, and then departed.

Almost immediately thereafter, Ilya and Pierre left London to join Alexander Salkind in the South of France for the Cannes Film Festival. Though films are screened and awards are given at the Festival, Cannes is basically about buying and selling, with deals constantly being made in the bistros that line La Croisette, on the beach, aboard sleek yachts or in one of the posh gaming houses. As one well-known London-based gossip columnist summed it up: "You really don't have to feel bad if you miss Cannes. Because despite all the fun, it's essentially a series of business meetings. Sure, everyone is in bikinis, but you can bet your ass they've all got mini-calculators tucked in them!"

"The 'Superman' production first came to the attention of the Cannes Festival about three years ago," Christian Le Hemonet, the Salkinds' French advertising coordinator, informed me. "But this year our plans are the most spectacular. We've hired eight planes with promotional banners, we've rented space for twenty very big posters for the walls of the Carlton Hotel and we've booked between seventy to eighty pages of advertising in the trade papers.

"Last year, when people still snickered that 'Superman' would never be made, I had a lot of problems at Cannes. Of course, looking back on it now, it was actually quite funny. I had hired a helicopter to take a huge 'Superman' billboard out to position on one of the big boats and just as the helicopter was hovering over the boat, the wind changed direction sharply. Well, dragging the heavy poster, the helicopter nearly crashed into the bay and the poster was sliced in two! So the next day the local headlines read: 'Superman Makes Big Splash at Cannes Festival'!"

As it turned out, 1977 was also a problem year at Cannes for poor Christian; two of the planes he had hired were grounded in the French Alps due to bad weather, and one that eventually *did* show up might have been better off in some hangar, as it trailed a huge banner proudly announcing the beginning of principal photography on "Superman," produced by Alexander *Salking*.

These mishaps only added to the already considerable publicity within the trade for the production. The Salkinds would have no trouble marketing the film in the territories outside Warner's distribution deal. It was now vital to keep the hype from getting out of hand, and to assure this Gordon Arnell was sent to Cannes.

"Overkill can be a real problem," Arnell observed before departing for the Festival, "especially with a very commercial property. The publicity, I mean. 'Love Story' worked. 'Gatsby' and 'Kong' didn't. It basically boils down to the fact that no one has a secret formula.

"My own formula is expediency, really. Films in production move so fast that to get anything right at all is a bonus. You don't have time to dwell on a decision. If you do it, you do it. If you don't, it's gone. 'Superman' is a bit different, though, because of the long shooting schedule. But on any picture, things happen quickly. When I was in Russia on a film not too long ago, I was deported. The real reasons are veiled"— Arnell was once a British intelligence agent—"but basically it was in reprisal for a Russian cameraman who had been fired. I guess I was unpopular, too, because I wasn't censoring the Western press. Anyway, a film like this one can be a publicist's dream—or a nightmare. It depends on what he wants to make it."

The unflappable Arnell shuffled some of the press releases on his desk and grinned. "Getting space in the fan mags isn't a publicist's function, I think—that's easy. Controlling it, shaping it, pacing it—from the start of production until it's ready for release—that's the tricky part. A lot of films have blown out early and lived to regret it. Others try to hide their light under a bushel, and then they never really emerge. It's very difficult to find the happy medium."

Gordon summed up: "Anyway, even with a very commercial property like 'Superman,' publicity is the least of the problems on a picture during shooting."

That was already visibly true—and it would be proved even more true in the months to come.

●　　●　　●

With the producers' departure for Cannes—Ilya left at the last possible minute, after waiting seven hours for the delayed arrival of his wife Skye and their daughter Anastasia from L.A.—the cast and crew of "Superman" settled into Pinewood and began work on the enormous *Daily Planet* set·on "E" stage.

Not since the recent "All the President's Men" had a major newspaper office been so carefully and imaginatively constructed for a motion picture (or, probably, for a real newspaper). An enormous illuminated ceiling, rows of glass-partitioned editorial offices, dozens of desks—and American office equipment was brought in by the ton to assure realism on the set. All this added to the complexity of the shooting; the little over two weeks that had been allotted for completion of the *Daily Planet* sequences stretched into almost five weeks of agonizingly drawn-out photography.

Part of the problem was the usual last-minute confusion over casting, when another down-to-the-wire situation developed over the selection of a Perry White, the slightly bumptious but loveable managing editor of the *Daily Planet*.

As the dates for Perry's appearance in the picture rapidly approached, Pierre returned from Cannes—Ilya stayed on with Alex to continue marketing the picture —to discuss the possibilities with Donner. Several major stars were mentioned for the role, including Walter Matthau, Jason Robards, Martin Balsam, Eli Wallach and Edward Asner. A few of the names were rejected; one or two of whom the part was offered couldn't come to terms with the producers about money.

Finally it seemed that Jack Klugman would be Perry. The "decision" was made on a Monday, and since whoever was playing White was scheduled to shoot that Wednesday, the production office informed publicity, wardrobe, and other appropriate departments that Klugman would be arriving the following day. But just as the producers' assistant, Maria Monreal, was calling Los

Angeles to confirm flight arrangements, Klugman's agent telephoned from California to state that in fact his client was turning down the part. In a panic, Maria relayed this news to Ilya and Pierre (who was now back in Cannes) only to be calmly informed that there was absolutely no problem, because their back-up choice for the part, Eddie Albert, had *tentatively* accepted terms to play White.

By this time the production staff in general—and Gordon Arnell, and the entire wardrobe department in particular—were in a state of utter confusion, as arrival plans and costume measurements shifted from minute to minute. (Production secretary Pat Carr had to keep telephoning Harrod's to change the name on the card accompanying the fruit basket being sent to the Inn on the Park Hotel to welcome the would-be White!)

On Tuesday afternoon, as Eddie Albert's height, weight, and chest and neck sizes were being telexed to Yvonne Blake and her people, and Maria was on the phone to L.A. booking his ticket, Albert's agent telephoned Pierre (back from the Festival again) that his client would accept the part but only *after* a substantial renegotiation of the fee.

With Perry White on the call sheets for the next day, Pierre decided that now was the right time to panic. Already late for an important meeting in London, he roared back to town in his BMW at ninety miles an hour, while Maria Monreal frantically placed seven calls from the car telephone: four to the States (one of which clinched Keenan Wynn for the part), two to the production and publicity offices back at Pinewood, and one to Alex and Ilya in Cannes. (Gordon Arnell later told me that when he met Wynn at Heathrow, the veteran film star and his wife told the publicist that they had had a tiring, though very pleasant flight from Los Angeles, despite the fact that their close friend Eddie Albert had apparently cancelled his reservation on the same flight at the last moment—and by the way, did

Arnell know *why* Eddie had been coming to London in the first place?)

But the Perry White story wasn't over yet. Despite Wynn's reasonable request for an extra rest day, preparations went ahead to shoot his initial scenes the morning after his arrival. The production offices reasoned that they were getting drastically behind schedule; Donner had had to film around Perry White for two days already.

So Wynn's measurements were hastily phoned in to Yvonne, and the severely fatigued sixty-one-year-old actor was rushed to the studio, made up, fitted for costumes and put through hours of lighting tests and still-picture sessions. At the end of this ordeal he began complaining of chest pains and had to be taken immediately to a London hospital, where he collapsed, suffering from extreme exhaustion. Luckily, Wynn's condition was nothing more serious—the first fears, of course, were that he had suffered a stroke or heart attack. Sadly, however, it was enough to prevent Wynn from playing the part. And in a real case of eleventh-hour casting, screen and television star Jackie Cooper was finally set for the role—and proved, to everyone's relief, ideally suited to the character of White. (At the time, I was having my own casting problems; production supervisor Bob Simmonds told me that my playing a copy boy in the *Daily Planet* offices, as I had been promised I could, might well put someone's nose out of joint at British Equity. But to counter my obvious disappointment, Donner assured me that he would get me into one of the Metropolis scenes—even if it had to be as a subway "flasher.")

Shortly after this, Ilya Salkind determined that the one right actress to play Superman's foster mother, Ma Kent (Glenn Ford was later signed as Pa Kent), was Joan Crawford. His note to call Crawford's agent had scarcely been entered in his appointments diary when he heard a radio broadcast announcing that she had died. The black-humor comments going around the set the next day made much of the notion that being cast for a part in "Superman" was, like cigarette smoking, dangerous to the health. (No one, at least not in Ilya's hearing, made any such jokes when Phyllis Thaxter was finally cast in the role. Miss Thaxter is Ilya's mother-in-law.)

Fortunately no such drama developed when Ilya locked up E. G. Marshall for the part of the President in "Superman II," after considering Henry Fonda, Douglas Fairbanks, Jr., and—*my* suggestion—Gerald Ford.

•   •   •

From the very outset of filming on the *Daily Planet* set, the crew was besieged with problems. The design of the set—necessary to create the look of a crowded, bustling newspaper office—meant setting up each shot in cramped, close quarters. A particular nuisance were the many glass-partitioned cubicles; Dick had to make sure the cameras were set up in such a way as to avoid unwanted reflections.

A few days into the shooting, the tremendous demands made on the studio's generators by the extensive lighting needed for the set caused a massive blow-out on the main power line in Iver, effectively burning out even the back-up generators. This put the production another two days—and in Pierre's words, "tens of thousands of dollars"—behind schedule. (I later learned that while insurance did not cover accidents of this nature, the studio would be obliged to give the production an extra day's use of the stage.)

I took advantage of the break in filming to watch a portrait-photography session with Valerie Perrine that began right after lunch and continued until seven in the evening. A real pro at playing to any camera, Val stopped only to change wigs and elaborate costumes, and to switch tapes on her cassette recorder—the music helped her move better, she said.

On the ride back into town, Valerie playfully told me that I could conduct an interview—on condition that I massaged her aching feet while I asked the questions. This is not standard interviewing practice, but don't knock it until you've tried it.

"I'm excited about playing Eve Teschmacher. She's so deliciously tacky," Valerie giggled as I worked on her right arch. "I mean, even her name is tacky. Look at the way she dresses. Is that gauche or is that *gauche?* Really!" Valerie, who had arrived at Heathrow with fifteen pieces of luggage, grinned. "That's why I can enjoy the part, because there's little of Eve in me. I'm just a bit tacky, don't you think, darlin'? Anyway, it's good to be enthusiastic about the part you play. And I think 'Superman'—this whole movie—is going to be marvelous. It's a drag to be in something you don't give a damn about. But this is just marvelous! Why didn't someone think of doing it before?"

I switched to her other foot.

"My family is from Galveston, Texas. And from the time I was a kid, I knew I wanted to perform. I always did. I don't think I was very much appreciated at school as I was growing up because I was, shall we say, kooky. You know, I dyed my hair too soon and I wore too much make-up too soon, that sort of thing. But I didn't race off to Hollywood. I didn't try to meet all the right people. I never tried to do the right thing just to get into Hollywood. I just told myself, 'I want to be a movie star—and I'm going to be one!' and that was it. I believe in the power of positive thinking. And a helluva lot of hard work!"

Then, in her usual coquettish manner, Valerie abruptly changed the subject. "Do you know what I'm planning to do after 'Superman' is released?" she asked. "I'm going back to Vegas and do a topless act!"

In her best mock Scarlett O'Hara style, Valerie fluttered a hand in front of her face like an imaginary fan. "My, my, my," she gushed. "I *am* naughty!"

• • •

Thomas Edison, who started the whole movie business when he invented the motion picture camera, used to attribute his success to the magic formula: "Ten per cent inspiration, ninety per cent perspiration." Chris Reeve was proving this all too well, giving costume designer Yvonne Blake a new problem.

After a few hours under the broiling lights on the set, Chris, decked out in his majestic Man of Steel duds, would be sweating profusely. During a take, when the moment came for Superman to stretch his arms and go soaring off into space, Reeve would assume the appropriate posture, thereby revealing large, rapidly spreading perspiration stains. Somehow the thought of Superman sweating like any mere mortal was decidedly disquieting, but the problem was solved easily enough when the make-up department recommended some industrial-strength antiperspirant, and extra lining and dress shields were put under the arms of Chris's costumes.

Sweaty underarms weren't the only problems Chris was having with the famous togs. The supertight red tank-suit pants he wore over the blue leotard revealed some obvious protuberances—and not always in exactly the same place, which must have driven prim Elaine Schreyeck bananas, particularly when light-hearted members of the unit asked her each morning, "Was Superman 'dressed' to the left or the right when we wrapped yesterday, dear?" This problem, too, was easily solved: Yvonne ordered a large swimmer's cup to be worn under the pants, an idea Ilya liked because he thought it would enhance the supermacho image of Superman.

With the Cannes Festival over—happily, "Superman" had been the most talked-about production—and the producers back on the scene full-time, shooting continued at a snail's pace on the *Daily Planet* set.

Word had been pouring in from New York and

Hollywood about the newly released "Star Wars," obviously the hit of the season. The producers and the director reacted by beefing up the commitment of the "Superman" production to achieve the highest-quality special, optical and visual effects, despite the staggering cost and time.

This was a courageous step, considering that the film was now about three weeks over schedule, that Wally Veevers and the flying unit were encountering crisis after crisis, that the main unit was bogged down on "E" stage, and that Donner and the producers were constantly quarreling, blaming each other for the difficulties.

Luckily for everyone, a much-needed respite came with a break in the shooting to mark the national holiday honoring the Queen's twenty-five years on the throne.

The Silver Jubilee celebration in Great Britain that June was a stirring event, particularly for a visiting American. The ceremonies began with Her Majesty lighting an enormous bonfire, the first of a chain of fires, each within sight of another, all across the island. The next morning, thousands of people gathered throughout London—men, women and children decked out in Union Jacks, banners and badges. And everywhere hung portraits of the Queen and Prince Philip, bordered in red-white-and-blue bunting.

The day's festivities concluded with a nationwide series of block parties and back-yard barbecues, including a lovely one given by Ilya Salkind's personal secretary, Sue Hausner—with hearty English sausages standing in for our traditional hamburgers and hot dogs.

This brief festive interlude did not lessen the "Superman" company's problems. The situation between Donner and the producers had deteriorated badly over the past few weeks, particularly since the main unit had been shooting on the *Planet* set. Recriminations were being slung back and forth at a dizzying rate, and there was talk of legal action from both sides. Ilya and Pierre claimed that Dick's slow, methodical pace—taking each shot from just about every possible angle—would bankrupt the production. Donner, on the other hand, accused the producers of trying to make major cutbacks that would threaten the success of the entire project. Sadly, as the tensions mounted and the atmosphere became more "political," lines were drawn, people split up into camps, and an attitude of "us against them" developed.

Loud shouting matches took place in Pierre's office between the producers and the director; Ilya and Pierre stopped visiting the sets; and finally Pierre refused to appear at all with Donner.

Then Alexander Salkind decided to telex Donner's attorney in New York, claiming that on the basis of the present schedule Dick was in breach of contract—and plans were made to replace him as the director of "Superman."

In spite of the problems they were rumored to have had with him on the "Musketeers" films, one of the first people the Salkinds and Spengler approached was Richard Lester, the accomplished director of many other films, among them "Petulia," "A Hard Day's Night," "Help!" and "A Funny Thing Happened on the Way to the Forum." The hope was that Lester, known to be a fast worker, would recoup the lost time and bring the picture in on schedule, or nearly so.

Rumors flew, and criticism was leveled at both sides because of the lack of communication between the director and the producers. Finally, the senior Salkind, in Paris, backed down from the decision to fire Donner and decided instead to approach Lester to join "Superman" as, in effect, another producer, functioning as an impartial mediator between the producers and Donner.

By now, wire services all over the world were ticking with the news. Before Lester made known his decision, Rona Barrett broke a catty story on coast-to-coast television on her syndicated "Good Morning, America" broadcast:

"Well, the superstory of the 'Superman' saga just won't wait until the Man of Steel flies across the screen, because stories, are already flying across the Atlantic from the London location of the epic. Producers Ilya and Alexander Salkind reportedly tried to remove director Dick Donner from the project, a fact confirmed by his agency abroad. At stake—some of the millions budgeted to make this film the successful superpic Donner wants reportedly being held back by the Salkinds, who would prefer keeping the picture at a lower budget so they could have a heftier profit. But Warner Brothers, which has put up some of the thirty million dollars reportedly received by the Salkinds, told them that Donner stays or their money goes!"

Very little in Rona's story was based on fact. But to be fair, it would have taken Superman's x-ray vision to see to the bottom of what was really going on.

Richard Lester's arrival with the title of "producer" sparked further rumors that this was a first step in easing Donner out. That was not the case; and fully appreciating the awkwardness of the whole mess, Lester, when asked how his first day on the film had gone, replied with a cautious smile, "Well, Dick Donner just bought me a beer in the pub. So I guess that's upbeat!" In fact, during his entire tenure on "Superman," Lester carefully maintained a low profile, vowing never to interfere with a setup or a shot and keeping his visits to the stage to a minimum.

With things a bit calmer between the warring factions, the mood on the main unit improved slightly. Work progressed, though slowly, on the *Planet* set; and the production office, along with North American locations coordinator Timothy Burrill, who was already in New York, made plans for eight weeks or more of location work.

On the set, though, new problems still continued to

crop up every day. Because of the tremendous heat generated by all of Geoff Unsworth's additional lighting equipment, the temperature on "E" stage rose to over 100 degrees one day. The studio's automatic sprinkling system was activated, briefly dousing everyone on the set, creating general havoc, and damaging some of the set dressing.

And it appeared that I wasn't the only one risking problems with British Equity. Word reached the producers that two of the local extras in the *Planet* sequences had "discovered" that their services were being enlisted for two films, not just one. However, the cries of "foul play" were patently unjustified. It was well-known on the set that "Superman" I and II were being filmed simultaneously; and extras were paid at a daily rate, not by a lump sum, so that additional work meant additional days at additional pay. Fortunately, the potentially disruptive situation was efficiently dealt with by Bob Simmonds and the production office.

•　　•　　•

Since five separate units were shooting, and we were only days away from departure for location, I went into high gear gathering information for this book, stopping in on each of the sets for an hour or so, taping interviews and lunching with the crew or key members of the cast on the production team. One day, after a lunch with John Barry, I was taken on an eye-opening tour of the working quarters of the more than two hundred people who fell under the jurisdiction of the art department: sculptors, designers, painters, draftsmen, plasterers, carpenters and the like, each group with its own workshop or block of offices.

The last week before we left England was even more hectic than usual, with everyone on the main unit trying to complete the scheduled work before the July 3 departure date. Marc McClure, a young Californian

resh out of the Disney hit "Freaky Friday," showed up
hat week to put in a few days in the role of cub reporter and photographer Jimmy Olsen. (He would
eturn later in the schedule to complete his stint.) For
his quintessential innocent, complete with curly hair
nd freckled face, Jimmy was surely a clear case of
ypecasting—it seemed appropriate that Marc's contract
precluded him, for however long he continued to por-
ray Jimmy Olsen, from appearing in any film, "in-
olving nudity or sexual acts"!

"You know, this is my first trip abroad," the twenty-
ear-old actor told me, looking slightly apprehensive.
And coming to England to work in a film like this is
eally fantastic! I watched a lot of television when I
eally was a kid and I loved 'Superman.' Little did I know
hen that one day I would *be* Jimmy Olsen. Wow!"

Marc's enthusiasm was mirrored by E. G. Marshall,
who chatted with me for half an hour after completing
is three days on the picture.

"Oh yes, I remember Superman quite well from my
ounger days," Marshall recalled, smiling. "Americans
ave always been interested in space . . . in what lies
out there,' so to speak. I guess this is an interest that
: really world-wide. The idea that space is limitless,
nfinite, seems to bother people. The possibility that life
xists outside our solar system is strong, and people
re very curious about it. Eventually, one day, we'll
make contact with that life, and I think that's part of
he attraction of Superman . . . the chance—the hope,
ven—that there *is* a superbeing, a form of superman;
hat there *is* an intelligence greater than our own out
here.

"We all grew up with Superman, so he's very much
part of our lives. I think he has more appeal than
Mickey Mouse, actually! Because Superman is human,
nd yet he's *superhuman*. As Clark Kent, he's just like
ou and me. And it's the Clark Kent in all of us with
which we identify. We'd all like to have that feeling

that we are immortal, that *nothing* is impossible for us.'

The last Saturday before we left, after spending the morning in my office trying to make sense of my growing mountain of notes, I decided to devote the balance of the afternoon to main-unit shooting and took the short walk between the administration block and "E" stage. Ignoring the red shooting light over the stage door—perhaps because the automatic door locking system, which usually goes into operation when the shooting bell is sounded, had not been activated—I walked behind the enormous set, thinking that it was amazingly quiet, and mounted the back stairs and strolled out into the *Daily Planet* offices. Noting casually that all the extras were in their proper places, at their desks, I glanced appreciatively at the details of the set dressing—authentic American newspaper clippings, photos, posters of Joe Namath, Bella Abzug, Robert Redford and the like. Suddenly my eyes were drawn by movement at the far right corner of the stage. Turning slowly, I saw Dick Donner, Ilya Salkind, and the entire camera crew gesticulating frantically in my direction. The blood rushed to my face as I realized that I had just walked into the middle of a take! I stood there, frozen. For a long, agonizing moment, the only sound was the whirring of the camera; then an anguished Donner threw up his hands and yelled "Cut!" waited to see who'd blow up first, betting on Ilya, the most mercurial man in the limelight this side of Idi Amin Dada. Instead, the entire unit, extras and all, erupted in laughter as Salkind bellowed with mock gruffness, "I'll be sure to put the eight-thousand dollar '—a rough estimate of a ruined take—' on your bill!"

●　　●　　●

America's much-loved "Kid," Jackie Cooper, shares his thoughts about playing America's much-loved boss

Perry White, before he finished his bit and jetted back to Los Angeles.

"I think Perry is like a lot of newspaper editors I've met—dedicated to the business more than to anything else," Cooper reflected, his face still stamped with the boyish good looks that had been his trademark forty years before. "Because he was a reporter himself and has grown to be an editor, he's even more passionate about the newspaper business than a reporter. He considers himself a leader—at least as far as everyone on the paper is concerned—so he feels responsible. And to Perry White, responsibility means authority and having people under his thumb. Not in a negative way, mind you, but in a caring, protective way. For all that surface gruffness, underneath, I think, like the script says, 'he loves his grandchildren.' He certainly has a warm spot for a new kid like Clark Kent—and yes, he is a humn being. But he does get very dramatic about things, and doesn't realize that sometimes he's a very corny character, complete with all the cliches."

Jackie wrapped, and the production finished nearly five arduous weeks on the *Daily Planet* interiors, with the progress reports showing that they had completed only one or two shots each day. On most feature films, a main unit can hope to get between two and a half and three and a half minutes of useable screen time in the can per shooting day. On the *Planet* set, Dick had been fortunate to get a daily average of forty seconds or less. (This, however, was not in fact the nadir of the production; that came late in the fall during one very grim week, when four full-time shooting units at Pinewood turned in a daily screen-time average of *eight seconds.*)

•　　•　　•

Since an easy day's shoot was scheduled and everyone needed a release from the tensions of the previous month, Dick Donner arranged a triple birthday party on the set for Elaine Schreyeck, Geoff Unsworth and Peter MacDonald, complete with a big cake. Enthusiastic as ever, despite the weeks of severe physical and emotional strain, Dick was able to joke about the trials he'd been through. Spying an unidentified man in a dark suit wandering around, he cracked: "Hey, what's this? Is Salkind sending in the heavies to drag me off the set?"

However, strangers milling around the closed "Superman" stages did put the producers in a panic, prompting them to huddle again with Gordon Arnell and come up with a new set of "Superman Security Procedures." The new embargo on outsiders covered: 1. Rushes; 2. Press visitors; 3. Company visits; 4. Personal visitors; 5. Photographers; 6. General photography; 7. Television coverage; 8. Story; 9. Special effects (which caused the greatest consternation); 10. Reference material; and finally, 11. Non-"Superman" personnel. It is interesting to speculate on what might have happened if the Queen or Prince Philip had wished to visit the set—"Catch-11" would seem to rule them out.

These new guidlines, distributed to the entire production team, ended with the footnote that "the recent and immediate success of 'Star Wars'—the blockbuster of the year so far—on which some of you worked, has reinforced our views that to be able to complete this project quietly, sensibly and without any outside fuss would be beneficial to us all."

Because the main unit was practically on its way to the airport, the producers added: "In due course we shall set up a separate system to be adopted for the North American locations. Thank you for your cooperation."

•　　　•　　　•

The day before we departed for New York, the major English trade paper, *Screen International*, ran a front-page story claiming "Too Many Foreigners Being Trucked in on 'Superman'"; I passed a kidney stone (which Dick Donner suggested I contribute to the lunar surface set being built for "Superman II"); and the general nervous hysteria that characterizes the departure of any major film production for location work prevailed. Despite the pressure of last-minute details, the director, as enthusiastic as ever, made his round of the units (second unit, model, matte and flying) remaining at Pinewood, slapping backs and booming out, "Atta boy!" or "Keep up the good work, baby!" I left him laughing that evening when I told him that I had written a special press release for the States explaining Richard Lester's position on the production, headlined: "Only 'Superman' Has Two Dicks!"

We said our farewells, packed up what personal gear hadn't been shipped ahead, and left Pinewood for at least the next six weeks. Next stop . . . Metropolis.

7
"We'll see Manhattan"...
sort of

One of the great reasons for working in the film industry is the lure of location shooting. With today's blockbuster productions, backed by ever-increasing budgets, places like Hong Kong, the Antarctic, Tahiti and Rio are on the itinerary, when once the studio back lot was as far as a film crew could expect to travel.

In the weeks, months—years, in fact—before principal photography began on "Superman," the producers had boasted to their own people, as well as leaked it to the trades, that the colossally budgeted film would be circling the globe to shoot in such glamorous far-off locations as Australia, South America, Ethiopia, and possibly China. Of course, even with a production like "Superman," reason and practicality occasionally prevailed. Somehow the bulk of the shooting turned out to be done at Pinewood and Shepperton, only a stone's throw from "exotic" Iver Heath, Fulmer and Slough!

But for the twenty to thirty-odd English members of the main unit who were heading across the Atlantic (costs and American union restrictions precluded using more than that number), the next two weeks of shooting meant working on one of the most exciting film sets anywhere—the island of Manhattan.

The crew left England in shifts over a three-day period, July 2 to 4, which meant that some of them would get a taste of our own annual jubilee celebration

—Independence Day—before shooting began in New York.

New York may be a summer festival, as the municipal posters claim, but the atmosphere was more like a Roman circus than first steamy day on the set—midtown Manhattan on 42nd Street between Second and Third Avenues, a sweltering contrast to the air-conditioned hotel in which the unit was headquartered.

The shooting in New York opened with the *Daily Planet* exteriors, and arrangements had been made for the New York *Daily News* building to fill in for the Metropolis newspaper.

As preparations were being made for the shooting, New York production coordinator Chris Coles took a moment to share with me some of the odder pre-production experiences of the New York team.

Ruth Morley, a well-known costume designer who had just completed work on "Annie Hall" and had been shuttling back and forth across the ocean to assist Yvonne with the American wardrobe, had arranged to go to the White House a few weeks earlier to sketch and photograph the uniforms of guards and other background detail. Instead of being asked to produce proper documents and security clearance, Ruth was given free rein to wander in and out of offices in the Executive Mansion at will—and she wound up in the Oval Office itself, with Jimmy Carter sitting at his desk. After apologies and some clarification, an astonished Ruth was permitted to leave with her photos and notes.

Chris also let me know:

• that a twenty-ton cabin cruiser from New Jersey, booked for a particular sequence, had to be brought into the city via the George Washington Bridge—the only bridge linked to Manhattan big enough to accommodate it—and even that had to be closed to other traffic to make way for the boat!

• that the fleet of trucks hired to serve as *Planet* de-

livery vans were actually *New York Post* delivery trucks
. . . and here we were at the New York *Daily News!*

• that two *Daily News* critics, Rex Reed and Kathleen Carroll, were set for walk-ons in the *Planet* shots.

• that New York unit coordinator Bob Colesberry spent a good part of the week before filming began getting to know every owner, operator, supervisor, janitor and cleaning woman in the *Daily News* building to arrange for the lights to be switched on in the appropriate office windows each night of the shooting, to the tune of about $2,000 a night (it was $7,500 a night later on Wall Street), which must have made Con Edison very happy.

• and that young newspaper hawkers arrived on the scene just prior to the shooting to hand out copies of a sleazy-looking newspaper entitled the *Daily Planet*.

All the people involved with the production had their photographs taken and were issued clip-on identity badges with name, Social Security (or hotel-room) number, and the signature of Peter Runfolo, the New York production manager. Despite this precaution and other high-powered security measures, the news that "Superman" had landed in the city meant that the set near 42nd Street would be constantly crammed with onlookers and gate-crashers, plus about 100 to 150 members of the working press—including TV, radio, newspaper, magazine, freelance and foreign correspondents—in addition to the regular film crew and a crowd of truck drivers.

The filming in front of the *Daily News* building demonstrated some of the problems of location work in the Big Apple, particularly in the summer. Despite weeks of preparation and an army of English and American assistant directors, the sidewalks were jammed with pushing, milling crowds. Curious drivers blocked traffic and often-belligerent bystanders ignored—or sometimes challenged—the production personnel who tried to keep things moving. Add to this the stifling, humid weather.

Needless to say, things didn't move any faster on the sidewalks of New York than they had on the stages at Pinewood Studios.

•   •   •

Like most people with film units on location, we spent our evenings off seeing the sights or bitching about the accommodations or counting the days till we could go home. At the end of a day's shooting in the muggy heat, it was a pleasure to jump into a unit car or taxi (with all those great New York prohibitions: "Driver cannot change more than $5," "Stop! Window will not go any lower," "No smoking," and "Please do not slam doors"), race back to one's room and dive into a bath or shower. The English crew often opted for staying in and watching American television. Their opinion: high on quantity, low on quality.

The second week in New York, we started shooting with Ned Beatty (Otis) in Grand Central Station, beneath which Lex Luthor has his subterranean lair. And if everyone had thought that working on 42nd Street had been hell, now the filming was moving down to the seventh level!

Most of the shooting took place in the cavernous central foyer and on Track 41, one of the unused rail lines at the station. The production staff had gone through a mountain of red tape to set up the shooting at Grand Central, and the city departments dealing with visiting film productions had all been helpful and cooperative. The commuter confusion resulting from Geoff Unsworth's need to have all the clocks, including the huge center one, stopped at 7:10, surprisingly placed no apparent strain on this cooperation.

Ned Beatty, one of the most talented and down-to-earth stars in films today, arrived on the set wearing a straw boater, striped shirt, white socks and plastic basketweave brown shoes, Yvonne Blake's imaginative concept of Luthor's hapless henchman. But as one might expect in New York City, in a matter of moments a wizened man wearing almost exactly the same outfit passed by the set. So much for Yvonne's creative inspiration—art does mimic life at times, even without meaning to.

Since the scene called for Otis to disappear through a trap door in the wall alongside the track just as a train whizzes by and a policeman tailing Otis is killed, the setups were intricate and the going was painfully slow, the whole business complicated by the terrible heat and foul air filled with smoke, both real and artificial.

Making use of Ned's natural sense of humor, Dick Donner added an extra establishing shot of Otis being tailed into Grand Central by the two detectives, stopping at a blind's man concession and stealing a bagel (Donner had the actor eating in nearly every shot), at which point the concessionaire's watchdog barks angrily.

After several days in the steambathlike depths of Grand Central, the unit moved back to 42 Street for additional shooting outside the *Daily Planet* (neé *Daily News*) building. An enormous crowd had gathered by early afternoon to watch stuntwoman Ellen Bry's spectacular jump—actually more of a bounce—from the awning over the *Daily Planet* entrance into a well-stocked fruit pushcart.

Later that day, before filming wrapped, Mayor Abe Beame, attending a meeting in the *News* building, came out to shake hands with Margot and Chris, welcoming Superman to Metropolis in an impromptu curbside news ceremony.

●　　　●　　　●

On Wednesday, July 13th, the "Superman" crew was instructed to rest in preparation for extended shooting that evening. Most of the British crew disregarded or-

—114—

ders and took advantage of the spare time to shop, sight-see and find ways to spend money. They would have been better off resting. . . .

The weather that day was normal for the time of year in the mid-Atlantic region of the eastern United States. The morning was hot and steamy; then the humid air combined with carbon monoxide and a pot-pourri of other pollutants to produce a thick, sooty haze that hung over the city until late afternoon.

We arrived at the *Daily News* building early in the evening. By six o'clock the block was swarming with film technicians, policemen, teamsters, extras and crowds of curious onlookers.

On the set, the usual pre-shooting preparations were going on—Geoff Unsworth and his New York counter-part Sol Negrin organizing the lighting, the assistant directors briefing the crowds on the gist of the scene, Chris and Margot in their vans getting into make-up and costume. And then at 9:38 P.M., Manhattan disappeared into pitch blackness!

Initial shock, incredulity, amusement and slight panic gave way to the overriding need to know what the hell had happened. Soon radio stations on back-up power systems were broadcasting the first sketchy details of what had caused the sequel to the Great Blackout of 1965.

The area of sustained, intense heat—the thermometer had still read 89 degrees at 8:30 P.M.—had been im-pinged on by an approaching cooler front, and the en-suing electrical storm had caused a lightning bolt to strike one of Consolidated Edison's key transmission lines, knocking out all electricity in the five boroughs of New York and Westchester County, and plunging some ten million people into darkness. One of the few bright spots that remained in Manhattan was the "Super-man" set, were Geoff Unsworth's brutes and mini-brutes continued burning in the midst of the eerie blackness, thanks to the unit's mobile generators.

—115—

At first the production officials in front of the *Daily News* building were extremely uneasy about the possibility that, given the tremendous drain on the city's power supply due to round-the-clock air-conditioning, the extra lights the production had had switched on in several buildings around the set might have triggered the blackout. If so, it would have been hard to compose a really effective apology. Luckily, news of the electrical storm absolved "Superman" of guilt.

Most of the crew, New Yorkers and British, tried to make light of the situation—pun intended. Someone suggested a headline for the next day's papers: "LEX LUTHOR LOSES LIGHTS." Raymond Walters, the editor of the paperback section of the *New York Times Book Review,* my guest for the evening's shooting, walked up to Chris Reeve and deadpanned, "All right, Superman . . . *do* something!"—a theme echoed in many local papers the next day. Actually, thanks to the film unit's generator and lights, the *Daily News* was able to go to press early that morning, so in a way "Superman" *did* come to the rescue.

Another visitor to the set that merorable night, Sol Harrison, president of DC Comics, wanted to call his wife in Queens to make sure everything was O.K. at home. He ducked into a phone booth in front of the *News* building, put in his dime, and . . . nothing. The lines were dead. Sol stood frantically clicking the receiver until he realized that he was standing in a dummy booth set up for the picture!

From what we heard on the radios at first, a light-hearted mood prevailed in the city, with people pouring out into the streets, dancing to portable cassette players, laughing, talking to neighbors they had never spoken to before, exchanging rumors, directing traffic, helping one another. Some kids were even setting off leftover Fourth of July fireworks. Apparently, it was 1965 all over again.

Not so. 1965 was a dozen years before. And the Big Apple had almost gone bust in the interim. It was a poorer, angrier, more frustrated city on that sweltering summer night; and as the hours wore on, the mood altered noticeably. Instead of dancing in the streets, people started calling out: "What's happening, man?" "I'm hot as hell!" "I hear the power won't be on until *tomorrow* morning!" "There's looting up in Harlem!"

At 10:30 p.m., as Tim Burrill of the production staff made a frantic attempt to check out the insurance situation (with the "force majeure" clauses and an "Act of God" later determined as the cause, the evening cost the producers only about $25,000, not the possible $250,000!), the crew broke for dinner, filing into a hot, sticky, empty storefront that had been set up as a makeshift dining room. After gobbling some sandwiches and a couple of sodas, I joined Skye and Ilya Salkind and Monique and Pierre Spengler in a van assigned to take us back to our hotels. We were soon joined by Donner, Tom Mankiewicz, Margot Kidder, sound mixer Roy Charman, and a number of others.

The journey in the van was enlivened by radio accounts of how chaos was beginning to grip the city—looting, fires, arrests. New York, it seemed, would have been better off that night with Superman on hand.

When we got back to the hotel (un-air-conditioned, of course), we joined hands and followed Roy Charman with his flashlight up the back stairs, single file, so that people could be dropped off floor by floor—the luckless Spenglers were on the seventeenth. Poor Roy Field got his key from the desk, groped his way to the eleventh floor and had to grope his way back down again. Wrong key, he told the desk clerk with proper English politeness.

After what shreds of a night's sleep the heat and humidity and noise from the street below allowed, we were greeted with the news over the radio that New York was a city under siege, with hundreds of policemen injured after battling looters—whose numbers were so great that the Tombs, the derelict men's detention center in lower Manhattan, had to be re-opened and was now filled to overflowing to accommodate the incredible number of arrests.

I was embarrassed to face my British friends at breakfast that morning. Many stories of kindness, sacrifice and bravery emerged out of that long, dark night. But it was the bad stories that stuck.

An outraged Mayor Beame held a press conference, demanding a full investigation into the power failure to determine just why the massive outage had occurred. Con Ed chairman Charles Luce had assured New Yorkers just four days before the disaster that he could "guarantee that the chances of a brownout or a blackout are less than they have been in the last fifteen years and that the chances are less here than in most other cities in the United States."

By Friday morning, things were getting back to normal—for New York. The *Daily News* carried the headline "FIRES, LOOTING RAGE IN CITY: 3,000 Arrests, 132 Cops Hurt." (In 1965, there had been only 100 arrests.) The mayor lifted the state of emergency that he had declared two nights earlier; the 6,000 commuters trapped in subway cars and trains had been rescued, and the city was slowly cleaning up the mess.

The stark fact facing the "Superman" unit was that the picture was now even further behind schedule. And it wouldn't be the last time that Mother Nature and Fate would join forces to stomp "Superman."

For the next few nights, the unit continued shooting at the Fulton Market, the famous fish-trading center of the city. Here the work was made memorable by the ripe odors and the winos who kept staggering up to crew members, saying "Hi"—hiccup—"I'm S-S-S-Superman!"

To make up for lost time, Dick split the crew into two units. The second unit shot the boat sequence not far away in Wall Street. I stopped by that location about one o'clock in the morning just as several extras dressed as hookers were complaining to the assistant directors that they were being solicited by some very unsavory-looking men.

Noticing Skye Salkind standing by a fire hydrant (needed to wet down the cabin cruiser so that it would appear to be dripping after being plucked from the East River by Superman), I strolled over to chat—and just missed being knocked off my feet as the hydrant cap burst, sending a stream of high pressure water across the set.

The next night, while an elaborate car chase and crash sequence was being filmed at the Fish Market, a real-life drama of the naked city was taking place. Vic Armstrong, the English stuntman, told me how the New York police had startled the film crew, who were packing up gear at 5:30 in the morning, by commandeering the boat, now back in the water, to rescue a would-be suicide who had jumped into the East River—once again, "Superman" to the rescue.

Before wrapping up on the Lower East Side locations, Dick decided to get a head start on a scene scheduled for a few nights later. So the crew moved to the rooftop of 111 Wall Street to begin a sequence—Lois Lane's departure by helicopter from the *Daily Planet* building —that ten months later would still be shooting at Pinewood Studios.

The next location was at 9 West 57th Street, the Solow Building, a massive, modernistic skyscraper of smoked glass and steel—an impressive setting for the first public appearance of Christopher Reeve as Superman.

At the Solow Building that night, the excitement was heightened by the street crowds and by the visitors who poured onto the set. Mario Puzo showed up to see his screenplay brought to life. Liv Ullmann, a long-time friend of Dick Donner, came to the set immediately after finishing her Broadway performance in "Anna

Christie." What with friends, relatives, and an army of reporters and photographers, the crowd was estimated to number in the thousands.

Reeve arrived on the set, looking understandably nervous, with three bodyguards, who proved to be unnecessary despite the mob. After disappearing into dressing rooms set up in the Solow Building, he emerged to be greeted by modest cheers, and began to rehearse the scene, in which Superman collars a burglar attempting to scale the building by means of suction-cup devices.

As make-up and wardrobe assistants made sure every hair was as it should be and every fold in the cape was correct, Yvonne Blake spoke briefly about Chris's costume. "I read somewhere that Chris is supposed to have twenty-five different costumes and six or seven special capes—for flying, crouching, leaping, sitting, standing, whatever. Actually, the number's probably higher than that. Mainly, that's where the wardrobe expense comes in, on all the doubles and duplicates and special-effects needs."

Chris was hooked into his flying rig, and then he was fastened onto the end of a giant Chapman crane.

Slowly, steadily, Chris was hoisted up into the clear night sky . . . and suddenly heads turned, traffic stopped and a spontaneous, thunderous burst of applause filled the air, followed by cries of "Mommy, mommy, look . . . it's SUPERMAN!" and "Hey, man . . . it's SUPERMAN!"

And it *was*.

Electrified by the crowd's enthusiasm, Chris broke into a broad smile, seemed to glow . . . and waved back enthusiastically at the crowd.

At that moment, surely, the producers must have realized that they'd probably have a hit on their hands. I know it took *me* five minutes to close my eight-year-old nephew's mouth.

●　　　●　　　●

The last two shooting nights in New York were on location in Brooklyn Heights—site of many a movie scene because of the unbeatable view of the New York horizon—and again on Wall Street.

The scene in Brooklyn, on a marvelous tree-lined street of brownstones, required Superman to rescue a cat from a tree—something a little less grand than reversing an earthquake in progress, but designed to demonstrate Superman's humility and humanity. Everything looked great—the location was great, Manhattan looked great, the flying rehearsals went great, the cape worked great and Chris looked great, despite the fact that he was eating a banana as he flew along.

Then the rain came, right after the dinner break. Frantic calls were made to Pierre—then the rain stopped. Just as the unit set up again, it started again. So, at 4:00 A.M., with everyone hot, wet and exhausted, the decision was made to wrap, leaving the scene unfinished.

Back at the hotel, the production executives were greeted with the news that the rushes had come in on Lois's helicopter sequence . . . and they were badly out of focus. These two scenes would now have to be rescheduled as pick-ups back in England . . . or somewhere else.

●   ●   ●

The producers gave a party at the hotel for the "Superman" main unit's last night in New York. Despite the oppressive heat—which had topped 100 degrees that day—there was plenty of laughter, boozing and good cheer as the English crew said goodbye to their New York "mates" and exchanged gossip, anecdotes and good-natured insults.

What had the London contingent thought of New York? "It's the most exciting city on earth," said one. "It sucks," said someone else. "I can't believe the eating in this city. It's fantastic!" exclaimed one of the camera crew. "It's the rudest, dirtiest, most decadent place on earth. If this is the Big Apple, then it's soft at the core!" said one of the production executives. Who needs a consensus, anyhow?

The next stop was Calgary, in the foothills of the majestic Canadian Rockies, for scheduled shooting of about four weeks.

Christopher Reeve as Superman

(Left) **The producers:** Pierre Spengler, Alexander Salkind, Ilya Salkind. (Right) **The director:** Richard Donner. (Below) Setting up a shot in Jor-El's laboratory.

(Top row) **Heroes:** Marlon Brando as Jor-El; Christopher Reeve as Clark Kent; Margot Kidder as Lois Lane.

(Bottom row) **Villains:** Gene Hackman as Lex Luthor; Ned Beatty as Otis; Valerie Perrine as Eve Teschmacher.

The infant Superman (Aaron Smolinski) astonishes Martha and Jonathan Kent (Phyllis Thaxter, Glenn Ford).

The Fortress of Solitude. Pinewood's huge 007 stage, bigger than a football field, is filled by the breathtaking set.

(Right) **One of costume designer Yvonne Blake's sketches of Marlon Brando as Jor-El.** *(Below)* **Make-up specialist Stuart Freeborn touches up a head mold of Christopher Reeve.**

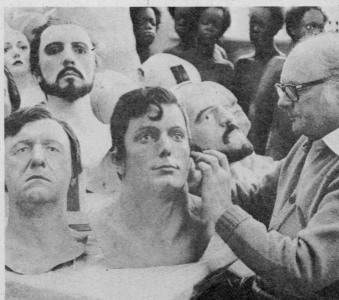

Models on the back lot of Pinewood Studios: *(top)* Boulder Dam is burst by an earthquake; *(bottom)* a replica of San Francisco's Golden Gate Bridge.

Men Who Made the Movie: *(top row)* Geoffrey Unsworth, Director of Photography; John Barry, Production Designer; Stuart Baird, Film Editor; Roy Field, Special Effects—Optics; *(bottom row)* Wally Veevers, Special Effects—Flying; Les Bowie, Special Effects—Models; Stuart Freeborn, Make-up.

Valerie Perrine
models her highly
personal T-shirt.

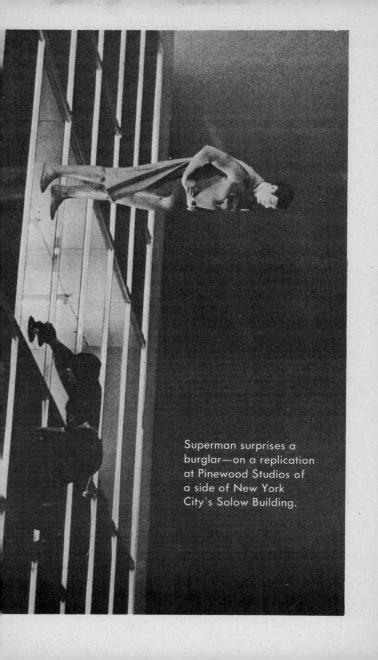

Superman surprises a
burglar—on a replication
at Pinewood Studios of
a side of New York
City's Solow Building.

A helicopter crash on the roof of the *Daily Planet* Building—and Lois Lane (Margot Kidder) hangs on for dear life!

8
Canada Dry is just
a soft drink

Once upon a time, estimates of the tab for the New
York shooting had been as low as half a million dollars.
When the figures were finally in, the two New York
weeks came to between 2.5 and 3 million. And the news
from Pinewood, to which Chris Reeve had already returned, was that the flying was going badly. The pros-
pects for a palatable budget and a summer 1978 delivery were becoming increasingly grim.

The location work in Canada, it was hoped, would
help cut costs, because of several economic advantages,
including the country's Commonwealth status, which
allowed most of the original main unit to work there.
But it seems to be a rule of filmmaking that there's no
bargain basement anywhere.

• • •

Calgary, Alberta, is much like a boom town in the
United States, with banks and office buildings rising up
out of nowhere to supply the needs of whatever industry created the town—in this case, oil and cattle. The
city lies on a featureless plain, but the majestic Canadian
Rockies provide a dramatic backdrop.

I checked into the Calgary International Hotel and
met up with Gordon Arnell and part of the featurette
(a documentary on the making of "Superman") crew.

They had just flown in from Sparta, Illinois, where they had visited the DC Comics plant. Then they had gone on to a little town nearby called Metropolis, originally planned as a Disneyland-style amusement center focused on Superman and his legend. However, the energy crisis, at its height as the town was taking shape, had stifled the enterprise.

As Arnell and his team were driving into Metropolis, they spotted an enormous water tower with a gigantic flying figure of Superman. After meeting with the mayor and receiving an honorary scroll as "supporters of Superman," the publicist and his film crew went back to the tower—and no Superman! Workmen had just finished taking it down to give the tower its annual paint job. Some quick and to-the-point talk with their friend the mayor got Superman reinstated, and the featurette team got the needed shot.

When the main crew pulled in, it was Old Home Week at the Calgary International, with the New York end of the English crew now reunited with old friends from the original main unit from Pinewood.

• • •

We were in Canada instead of Kansas, where the screenplay was set, because the growing season in Alberta was ahead of that in the States, and the wheat fields needed in the crucial scenes around the Kent farm were at just the right stage of growth for shooting.

After a rest day, the unit departed for a location shoot in Drumheller, about ninety miles away. I stayed behind to catch up on my notes and spent an evening with Ilya Salkind at "Moishe's—Calgary's Only Disco Delly."

I drove out the next day and joined the unit, busy shooting the cemetery sequence that follows the death of Pa Kent. The drive to Drumheller afforded some beautiful sightseeing—flat lands, rolling hills, pine forest, wheat fields, and occasionally cowboys, coyotes and even Indians—and the beauty of the location itself was particularly striking: sunburnt windswept hills fringed with rolling green pine forests. It was a perfect setting for the poignant cemetery scene in which Phyllis Thaxter and Jeff East come to pay their last respects to Pa Kent.

The church set in the background (built considerably less than normal size to give an effect of distance), the Stars and Stripes fluttering in the breeze, and the sun streaming through the high clouds made for a pure American scene right out of Norman Rockwell.

Later that week the shooting moved some sixty miles west of Calgary, halfway to the popular Rocky Mountain resort of Banff.

Gene Hackman, Valerie Perrine and Ned Beatty had by then arrived in Canada for about three weeks' work. (Margot Kidder, who was not as yet on call for any of the Canadian location work, had nevertheless chosen to take up quarters at a local resort ranch.)

The first morning on the new location, I drove out to the set with Skye Salkind and Valerie. All during the drive, Valerie calmly applied her make-up, including a set of fabulous false eyelashes, lash by lash—oblivious to the fact that we were in a unit car, bouncing along at 75 miles an hour. Sitting there in the front, hair in pin curls with a stocking over them to keep every curl in place, she went into her Scarlett act. "My, my, my," she said, fanning herself and eyeing the breathtaking scenery, "*all* this *and* thirteen thousand dollars a week too!"

The scenes being shot here dealt mostly with Lex Luthor's plot to waylay an XK 101 atomic missile convoy just long enough for his henchman Otis to sneak under the protective tarpaulins and tamper with the missiles' nagivational mechanisms. The crew spent the morning positioning a huge mobile home to block a nearby bridge (a plot point), so I spent much of that first day in the foothills of the Rockies chatting, swimming and sunbathing with Valerie. (While the two of us were off by a secluded lake, Valerie heard some noise in the brush behind us. From her sunning position, on her back, she tilted her head to see what the commotion was—and saw that she was only a few feet away from a pack of wild horses. "Don't panic," she whispered, "but there's a whole bunch of horses *without* people.")

Many of us wound up in Valerie's van at lunchtime; and because we could see that it was destined to be the "in" spot on location (how "in" can you be off the Kananaskis Highway?), I gave it the reasonably classy name of "Club S."

After lunch, I shaved off my mustache in preparation for the "Superman" part Donner had finally decided on for me—assistant football coach at Smallville High School. "I want you to get some sun on that upper lip, kid," Dick commanded, not without vindictive pleasure.

By the time the crew was ready to shoot, the rains came—a mountain storm of frightening intensity, complete with thunder and lightning.

Richard Lester had been sitting in Val's van telling us about his casting finesse: "I turned down Hackman for 'Petulia,' I turned down Redford early on for something else . . . so much for my insight into stardom." When the storm started, Lester stared glumly out of the van window, looking up at the forbidding clouds. "That sky can't be real," he said. "It's either a boardwalk painting on velvet or a Lithuanian potato carving."

Ilya Salkind sighed. "Do you know one reason we came to this part of Canada?" he muttered morosely. "The beautiful weather."

● ● ●

The next few days, at the Stoney Indian Reservation, were also weather washouts.

Because of insurance provisions, a film unit has to proceed with scheduled plans for shooting and hope that conditions will improve; only after a certain number of hours on the set can the first assistant director call it a wrap. I spent most of my time waiting around with Valerie, who, like every other principal scheduled to shoot on a given day, had to be in make-up, ready to go if the weather improved.

After several straight days of bad weather, we managed to get through part of the initial missile sequence, and the shooting broke for a three-day weekend. Most of the crew took off for nearby Banff, or Edmonton, or Vancouver—or even points in the U.S., including San Francisco and L.A.

Costume designer Yvonne Blake had to stay behind a little longer because of a new stunt scene Dick had just inserted which involved placing Valerie on a bridge over a canyon. Since Alf Joint would be doubling for Val, disguised in a blond wig, Yvonne had to whip up another matching costume, a form-fitting, slinky red dress, made to Alf's muscular measurements.

With Maria Monreal and Pierre Spengler's sister Katia (an assistant/trainee in continuity), I left for the famous Banff Springs Hotel, where we were later to be joined by Donner, Hackman, Valerie and Larry Hagman (the son of actress Mary Martin), who had just been cast in the role of an Army major at the missile base.

Banff is a popular Canadian resort town surrounded by cool pine forests, clear lakes and the majestic Rocky Mountains. Luckily for us, Valerie had brought Club "S" and her congenial driver Ken Cooper along, so we were able to take side trips. We spent our last evening at the hotel being serenaded on Valerie's terrace by two young lady bagpipers, complete with tartan kilts, reminders of the original Scottish settlers of the Calgary area.

After the extended weekend, the shooting resumed

with the missile sequence. The first morning back, I observed the stunt men and special-effects team as they set up an elaborate car crash involving a driverless remote-control car sent in by Lex Luthor as a diversion. After two aborted takes, the car did a fantastic double-flip and it was a print.

That afternoon, I drove back to town to witness a casting session for boys needed to play the young Clark Kent at various stages in his growth.

The session was held at the Calgary Inn Hotel. For several days, announcements had run in the local newspapers and over the radio that a number of Calgary boys would have a once-in-a-lifetime chance to appear "in the biggest motion picture production in history, 'Superman'!" Half the population of Alberta seemed to feel destined for the silver screen and hundreds of boys turned up. Some were perfect for the parts. Others didn't look even remotely close to what one would imagine young Clark Kent should look like as a child. Along with the cute kids, the whining kids, the wide-eyed frightened kids, and the kids oblivious to and unconcerned with the whole thing, came an army of parents who had decided that their Bobby or Billy was another Jackie Cooper redivivus. Some of them even brought their daughters, either misunderstanding the call or hoping that with a short haircut and just the right make-up, maybe. . . .

The whole circus had been left to Tom Mankiewicz and New York casting director Lou DiGiamo, who had helped out on the production in Manhattan and had films like "The Exorcist" and "The Godfather" to his credit. The final casting decision, of course, would be Dick Donner's. Mankiewicz and DiGiamo waded through the horde of applicants, who ranged in age from three to sixteen. Some of the kids were truly adorable and many of their parents were in fact friendly, low-keyed and cooperative. Many were not.

In the midst of all the chatter, crying and general commotion, one little boy kept walking up to Lou, asking, "Look, *when* am I going to be in this show?" (Lou assured me that even though the kid wouldn't be one of those selected, he'd probably end up as the agent for the kids who were!) Another child asked the bearded, slightly overweight DiGiamo, "Are *you* Soo-oooo-per-man?"

• • •

About this time, unsettling reports reached us from New York, where some members of the production staff were still wrapping up "unsettled business." The tales of woe concerned a legacy of unpaid bills, threats of broken kneecaps from some of the creditors . . . even a few cases of Mafia strong-arming.

While Pierre huddled with production coordinator Tim Burrill to try to sort everything out and delay as many creditors as possible, Ilya flew to Los Angeles to allay the growing fears of the distributor. He hoped also to have time for the more pleasant task of meeting with potential composers of the film score, and to begin working with the Warner advertising and publicity executives on preliminary plans for a "teaser" campaign (including leasing huge billboards in New York and L.A. and designing a *new* Superman logo for the film).

By this time, news of further delays had filtered back to the film community in California, and the pressures of meeting the shooting schedule as well as keeping the costs down became more intense.

The production's problems were not lessened by the fact that air traffic controllers in Canada had just walked off their jobs in a strike action. For a.d. David Tomblin, this meant additional headaches; he now had to make arrangements to get the artists in and out of Calgary via Great Falls, Montana. Ken Cooper, Valerie's Winnebago "captain," planned to drive Valerie, Ned Beatty and Larry Hagman, all of whom had finished their work in Canada, across the border to the States.

Before she departed, the ever-playful Perrine left Dick Donner her prize T-shirt, which had "Club 'S'" emblazoned on the front and a nude picture of Val, from an old *Playboy* article, on the back, accompanied by the legend, "Another day, another $300,000."

* * *

When the weather was good enough, the unit returned to the Kananaskis area to complete the Danforth Missile Base sequence.

During rehearsals on the set—crowded with hundreds of U.S. Army uniformed extras and snarling German shepherd dogs—cameraman Peter MacDonald noticed that the nose cone of the XK 101 missile was wobbling a bit. So David Tomblin asked me if I would get into the second stage of the rocket and hold the nose cone steady. Not quite sure he was serious, I agreed and proceeded to climb up onto the big flatbed truck. A moment later Alfie of Props came running over to say that I'd probably suffocate in there. "Don't worry," Tomblin chuckled, "we'd bury you over there on that hill under a marker that said: 'He Did It For The Book.'"

* * *

About this time, two very special members of the cast arrived for cameo appearances in the film.

Kirk Alyn, the original serial Superman, and Noel Neill, the first film Lois Lane (also the much-loved Lois of the TV series), had been suggested to Ilya Salkind by Rogers and Cowan publicist Dale Olsen as naturals to play the parents of Lois Lane in the new picture, in the scene in which she, as a little girl, sees the young Clark Kent speeding past a train. The young executive producer quickly locked up both Kirk and Noel for the parts.

Much to the amusement of most of us on the film, the two "Superman" veterans showed up in Calgary still reflecting some of the tensions that had apparently enlivened their earlier acting partnership, exchanging generally harmless barbs, still bickering about stolen scenes and stepped-on lines. They both looked great, Kirk tall and tanned, with a still enviable physique, and Noel as attractive and sparkling as when she first started at the *Daily Planet.*

"I *love* Noel," Kirk assured me, while Noel, sitting nearby, rolled her eyes. "When we worked together on the serials, she must have had an awful lot of faith in me. I carried this girl so many times through fire, through smoke, through all kinds of danger . . . and she'd dangle under one arm while I did these things. But she didn't mind, she didn't wince, she didn't even say a word. She just believed that I was Superman, and so I was!"

•   •   •

With a second Canadian unit leaving to shoot plates and additional scenes in the British Columbia icefields (these to be integrated later with scenes of Superman's Fortress of Solitude), the main unit headed south for what was then planned as three or four days of location work in the tiny town of Barons.

After getting a good night's sleep at the local Holiday Inn, we were up early—6:00 A.M.—for the drive to the set. Despite some ominous clouds, the weather forecasters had assured us that it would be clearing by late afternoon. Dick planned to devote the morning to rehearsals and get a shot in before wrapping.

The scene was a complex special-effects sequence that would be completed optically back at the studio. Young Clark Kent (Jeff East) would race past a thundering locomotive and then cross the track, leaping over the enormous engine at the instant it appeared that boy and train would intersect.

The train being used had been leased from Canadian Pacific at a cost of $5,000 a day, with the C.P.R. emblem painted over with "Kansas Star." This scene was another reason the production had decided on the Canadian location. The United States has, after several serious accidents during filming, made it almost prohibitive to use trains, and, more importantly, track lines (which is why, for example, the film "Silver Streak" was shot in and around Calgary).

To show Jeff running at super-speed past the train, everything had to be paced, timed and measured perfectly, so the rehearsals and setups were particularly painstaking and slow. And once again the weather had turned hot.

With Peter MacDonald's camera rostrum bolted onto the back of a truck, Johnny Richardson continually adjusting Jeff's flying rig, and Stu Freeborn checking the skin tones of Jeff's putty nose, Dick had a great deal to cope with. He would move them all off about two or three hundred yards down the dirt road from where he was standing and then shout "Action!" through his bullhorn. The truck would race toward him, the crane would —everyone hoped—keep Jeff barely an inch or two off the ground so that he'd appear to be running at an incredible speed, and the train would chug alongside down the track, gathering momentum. Then the truck would hang a sharp right onto the small gravel road crossing the track, and just as the train roared past, Jeff would be swung within a hair's breadth of the hurtling engine. Everything had been planned for and measured and tested to the limit. But just one error in the calculations—or someone's judgment—and Jeff East might have been up for a posthumous Academy Award.

Happily, Jeff survived.

●   ●   ●

Glenn Ford arrived to begin fittings for his role as Pa Kent and immediately voiced his intention not to wear a wig that had been designated for him. The adamant actor even went to Ilya Salkind, who wisely remained neutral, about the problem before finally taking it to Donner. Dick diplomatically asked his star to try on the wig—which had been hastily bought off a wigmaker's block in Los Angeles and hadn't been shaped or trimmed—then took one look and said, "It looks like Glenn Ford in a wig." So Pat McDermott whipped up a black water-based rinse for Ford's own hair (so that he could play Pa at an earlier age) which could then be washed out and replaced with gray highlights for the role of the older Pa.

While that imbroglio was going on, a second unit was detached from the main unit to start rehearsals on the scene with Noel Neill and Kirk Alyn. At least ten times the extras were loaded on the train, and ten times they were loaded off, as Dick ran through the paces with the two veteran performers and the little girl playing the young Lois.

Between shots, Kirk (whose business cards read: "Kirk Alyn—Superman") would reminisce about his days as the Man of Steel. "Superman has come a long way," he observed. "Even the famous costume has moved with the times. Now it's all latex and stretch material—it's beautiful. It sticks right to *you!* I was constantly stretching my costume and having to pull it into shape. You see, I wore a ballet costume when I was a dancer and they were wool and at least the wool was a good fit. But as Superman, my costume was cotton. The tights were cotton too, and before each take I'd stretch them out and then after each take I'd stretch them out again.

"I did just about all my own stunts too. In the beginning, for the tests, they had a stunt man, but the producer and the director realized it was no good. 'Kirk, the kids will never believe it. He doesn't look like you, he doesn't run like you . . . there's nothing about him that's like you!' they told me. So since I was very athletic, I did them all myself."

Kirk paused, running a hand through his still wavy hair. "I made two serials of fifteen episodes each. The first was in 1948, the second in 1950. 'Superman' was one of the last of the great Saturday afternoon serials. Sometimes, when I look back on it, I wonder whatever possessed me to do them. I was ready to quit on the first day, because the first day was, as kids say, 'the scariest thing that *ever* happened to me!'

"I had to prevent a train wreck by soldering the track with my x-ray eyes. And there we were in Los Angeles, in broad daylight, and there was no way to fake it. There I was, about two inches from the track as the train roared by . . . I'll never forget the feeling in my stomach!"

Noel Neill wasn't quite as enthusiastic about her work in the serials. But her attachment to the Superman myth was still evident.

"The serials were kind of the pits of the industry," she told me. "You mention serials today and people say 'Serials? What are they?' When I tour the college campuses, most of the kids I talk with have never seen or even *heard* of them.

"After the serials were over, the TV series started and the original producer didn't take me, he didn't take Kirk, and he didn't take Tommy Bond, who was the first Jimmy Olsen. But they switched Loises in 1953"—Noel's big hazel eyes flashed as they had when Clark Kent would annoy her—"and I went right through with George Reeves and Jack Larson until the series finished in '57.

"Looking back on it now, I realize just how hard we all worked. We did two shows a week . . . it was very fast and very time-consuming shooting. We worked from eight in the morning until eight at night; then we'd get our legal minimum twelve hours off and wham!—back again. It wasn't what I would call fun at the time . . . we didn't have outtakes and whatever. I think we printed *everything*.

"The special effects were crude in those days, compared to what we're doing now. George Reeves had several methods of flying—visually, I thought they were pretty good—and some of the mechanisms worked quite well. But nothing like what's being done in this movie.

"Jack Larson [Jimmy] and I flew in one of our shows . . . in fact, the last one we did. Jimmy gets hit on the head with a sandbag in this little professor's laboratory, and he dreams that the professor has invented a pill which we both take, and then we fly and we crash through the walls and bring the 'heavies' to justice. 'All That Glitters' was the name of that episode."

The call came for *my* big scene in the film. That morning, along with all the "dress extras"—footballers, cheerleaders, spectators, motorists—I picked up my costume at the El Rancho Motel and then departed for the gymnasium of the little red schoolhouse, where we were to change and get into make-up.

As an assistant football coach at Smallville High, circa 1950, I had to submit, in addition to the earlier mustache shave, to having my hair cut and Brylcreemed down. I improvised a bit, tucking a Fonz-esque cigarette behind my ear beneath my baseball cap.

While I was still in make-up and an a.d. came running in, saying that someone had mentioned that American football players applied blacking under their eyes so that the sun wouldn't reflect in them. I confirmed this—the British and the Canadians seemed unaware of the practice—and Stu Freeborn's assistant hurriedly applied heavy black make-up to the whole football team.

The first application looked like Indian war paint, so I quickly explained that it should be more like a finger-mark.

Not that I'm any expert on American football. Since the scene at the school was to open with warm-ups and other activity on the field (which had to be "cut" from part of the adjoining wheat fields and sown with grass seed especially for the film), Dick had me tossing the pigskin to three of the players. Now I know what Charlie Brown feels like. Tennis I play; football I don't —nor have I ever. After Donner had watched a few of my feeble tosses, I was relegated to working out with Jeff Atcheson, an accomplished athlete, who was play-ing the coach.

Donner bore me no malice, however, even going so far as to give me a line to say to Clark Kent, the team's water boy, as we left the field: "Hey, Clark, let's have all this leather washed and waxed for Saturday's game O.K.?" And to the coach: "G'night, Jeff." Plus a slap on the back and a leap over the bench—maybe.

Despite the dawn call, I was enough of a ham to love every minute of that first morning, though naturally was just a little nervous. I needn't have been. When we were almost ready to shoot, after hours of patient wait-ing, the dark clouds rolled in, the sun disappeared, and the rains came.

The next day dawned gray, chill and very wet. But regardless of the weather, everyone on call had to be out on the set as usual in case the weather changed

The bedraggled unit, cast and crew, hung around most of the morning, chatting, reading, listening to still photographer Bob Penn's jokes, or just plain moping. The dampness and cold seemed particularly penetrating after the stretch of warm days, and by evening we were all sniffling and sneezing, and the nurse was being be-sieged with requests for prescriptions.

The following day was gray again, but it was Sunday an off day, and most of the crew opted for spending in bed. Luckily, the weather cleared at the beginning of the week. They were ready at last to shoot the much-delayed football sequence.

Believe it or not, I had spent most of my Sunday off rehearsing my *line*—Stanislavsky and my high school drama teacher, Miss McMindes, would have been proud of me—and I arrived on the set mumbling the words over and over: "*Hey*, Clark . . ." No. "Hey, *CLARK* . . ." Yes!

I was still observant enough to notice the great costumes—all the "poodle" skirts Dick had specifically requested, the saddle shoes, the pegged pants—as well as the fantastic cars—a '47 Olds, a '50 Studebaker Hawk and assorted Chevys—that had been brought in for the scene.

Ed Finneran from Massachusetts and Tim Hussey from California, two boys who had won a DC Comics contest which offered parts in "Superman" as prizes, were on hand to appear as football players. They were out on the field at 7:00 A.M. sharp, tossing the ball under the watchful, and slightly bleary, eyes of their proud mothers.

Though the morning was sunny, they weren't ready to shoot until after lunch. (As it turned out, my four seconds of screen time required three takes and two afternoons, and months later I learned that the scene probably wouldn't make it into the final print!) The first take was truly memorable.

After running through the scene a couple of times, with Donner continually berating me for doing something wrong, a take was called for. I was still standing with Pat McDermott, who was making a few last-minute adjustments to my unruly hair, when Dick screamed "Action! Petrou . . . where the hell *are* you?!?" I went racing off, camera right, hardly waiting for my cue. But as I approached the point at which I was to deliver my line, I could see that my unobtrusive marker had been replaced by a huge wooden camera box. Not wanting to ruin another take on this problem-prone picture, I ignored the unexpected obstacle, stepped blithely up onto the crate and proceeded to deliver my line—at which point Donner and everyone else in the vicinity, including Jeff East and Jeff Atcheson, collapsed in hysterics. "Don't take it hard," counseled David Tomblin, who had switched markers while I was in hairdressing. "We figured that since we're shooting in Panavision, unless we raised you they'd only have seen a baseball cap walking across the screen!" I was sure my crimson face was shining through my carefully applied make-up. I cheered up a little when my old friend Roy Charman agreed to do a "wild track"—a special loop—of my line later in the afternoon.

That wasn't my only trouble with the scene. After delivering my sixteen words, I was to walk away, jump into a waiting Studebaker Hawk and drive off. With four cars on the field, why was I the only one who couldn't get his into gear? Finally, John Scott, in charge of transportation for the Canadian end of the production, was enlisted by Dick to be my driver.

The last two days in Barons were devoted to a special-effects sequence on the football field.

The final shot of the Smallville High scenes had an angry Clark Kent walloping the pigskin across the field and out of the stadium after having been put down by the school bully in front of Lana Lang, his first "romance." (Superman must have a thing for alliterative L's.) Of course, getting the football to take off as written took the better part of an afternoon.

John Richardson and his crew accomplished this by having a deep trench dug, and placing in it a long metal, cannonlike tube connected to a big air pressure tank. Into this mechanism were loaded painted wooden footballs—to provide the extra weight needed for the proper trajectory—which were then rocketed out across the field.

Dick was happy that during the shot, as well as in

the background of the previous scene between Clark and Lana, we got a free bonus of local color: a long grain-hauling freight train moving backward and forward on the track as it picked up harvested wheat from the Barons depot.

As we left the area, local school kids surrounded the unit with requests for mementoes and autographs—from Dick, the crew, the Canadian drivers . . . even me!

The day after our return to Calgary, we were all up for an earlier-than-usual morning call to drive the forty-odd miles to the Kent Farm location in Blackie.

Everyone was feeling the effects of the continual delays. Noel and Kirk, along with Ed and Tim, the two DC Comics contest winners, had been told that they'd be needed "for two days, at most," which had stretched out into a week. The additional delay in Barons because of bad weather was another serious financial drain on the film, as Donner and the producers were painfully aware.

The Kent farm location, a clapboard farmhouse and barn in a picturesque setting of wheat fields, had been thoroughly readied, thanks to the extra time, so there was hope that the shooting might move rapidly enough to pick up a day or two. Unfortunately, shooting did not progress this quickly, due in large part to the fact that so many key people, Donner included, were still suffering from colds and flu picked up standing around in the rain in Barons.

After the mob scenes in Barons, the "Kent farm" seemed blessedly quiet. Glenn Ford, looking relaxed and tanned, chatted with crew members; Phyllis Thaxter admired the set dressing—which included chickens, pigs, cows and calves.

Gordon Arnell and Bob Penn, along with special-effects man John Richardson, were on the Kent farm set most of that first week, coordinating an elaborate still-shot sequence which might possibly be incorporated into the film, detailing the growth and displaying the super powers of young Clark. Using the young boys selected at the earlier casting session in Calgary, Richardson had to create effects which included milking a cow at super-speed, chopping a cord of wood in a single blow, and lifting a tractor. Since these fantastic actions had to be depicted in still shots rather than in motion, the sequence provided Bob Penn with some unique problems.

While all this was going on in Blackie, a second film unit was heading north by helicopter for more shooting in the Columbia icefields and glaciers. Michael Green, acting as second assistant director in the second unit, was called upon to stand in for an absent Valerie Perrine as her lighting double and was listed on the Call Sheets under his "nom de cinema" Michel *Vert* (which means "green" in French!)

Decked out in Valerie's flamboyant red-orange–dyed Persian lamb outfit, complete with orange sunglasses, Michael almost got stranded on a glacier with a guide and Gene Hackman's fur-clad stand in. As ominous gray clouds dropped lower and lower, it seemed unlikely that a helicopter would be able to make its way through the jagged cliffs and ice peaks. And with the gaping chasms below, plus the threatening storm above, the three anticipated being stranded there for the night. Fortunately, however, a second 'copter was able to descend and pick them up.

After the initial shots on the Kent farm, the main unit moved to a dirt road between two nearby wheat fields to film the arrival of the starship carrying the infant Kal-El to Earth. In contrast to the order and organization on the farm set, here was a nightmare of chaos and confusion, brought on by a combination of altered schedules, added scenes, vehicular movement and inadequate planning—even in minor details; Phyllis Thaxter laughingly noticed that the name on her chair had been misspelled "PHYLIS."

Shooting commenced with a smudge-pot device giving off three magnesium powder bursts to create the smoke necessary to simulate the crash landing of the starship. The surrounding wheat field had been scorched and sprayed with black paint, particularly along a trench dug during the night. But when Dick arrived on the set, he decided the setup didn't look convincing enough, so the art department had to get to work again.

When everything seemed reasonably ready, Glenn and Phyllis, both in middle-America dress, circa 1940, got into a purplish '47 GM pick-up. The truck, with a preflattened rear tire, was backed up to a designated starting point from which Glenn was to drive toward the camera, while John Richardson dashed ahead with a smoke-making device so that the truck would appear to be throwing up dust on the dirt road.

After several rehearsals on this part of the sequence, Glenn was directed to stop the truck along the side of the road, get out and then, together with Phyllis, quickly turn and stare as the starship crashes into the field.

On the first take, poor Glenn couldn't get the truck's door handle to work. Then, after one successful shot, the brakes went completely, forcing him to steer the runaway pick-up into some sandbags and lighting equipment. Luckily, no one was hurt and there was little damage to the equipment. Glenn, a veteran of many westerns, remarked, "A horse I can stop. A truck's something else!"

Because of more lost time, the next day's call was an hour earlier on the dirt road location, but since the cloud patterns kept changing and the lighting was so variable —making it a nightmare for Geoff Unsworth to achieve matching shots—the unit wasn't ready for rehearsals until after eleven. So while Dick positioned himself in Roy Van Buskirk's Chapman crane (which Roy had driven the 1,600 miles from L.A.) for a wide-angle shot, I took the opportunity to chat with Glenn Ford and Phyllis Thaxter.

Sitting next to me in the tall grass alongside the road, with technicians milling around us, Ford looked ruggedly handsome and seemed unusually relaxed—despite the fact that he would be leaving for Los Angeles in a week to be married again.

"I'm glad to see that my friend Dick Donner—we've known each other for twenty-five years—is playing this film straight," he said. "Look at the part I play—Jonathan Kent—a simple, midwestern, salt-of-the-earth fellow. He knows his 'son' is extraordinary, that he's possessed of extraordinary powers. But he never really tries to figure it out. He says, 'Son, I know you're here for a reason. I just don't know *what* that reason is.' He treats Clark as normally as possible and he wants him to grow up like other children, with honest, basic values. I think that's the secret to this whole show . . . playing it very, very honestly, not playing against it. That's what Dick wants. To make it as real as possible so that people can say, 'Hey, maybe such a thing *could* happen.'

"Look, I don't mean to make it more than it is. This film is pure entertainment. We have enough violence and obscenities in our lives. People will see this film and be entertained. And that's what this business is for!"

Phyllis Thaxter, a strikingly handsome woman even in her Ma Kent make-up, agreed with Ford. "I'm thrilled with the magic and excitement of this film, and I feel very much a part of Ma Kent," she said. "Now that I'm into the character, that goes for *everything*—the shoes, the stockings, even the old-fashioned undergarments. I guess I feel like 'Earth Mother'!

"My children idolized Superman," she recalled, perhaps mindful that she was speaking not only as one of the stars of the film but also as the executive producer's mother-in-law. "They used to buy all the comic books and watch the television show. I can remember Skye running around the house with her blanket saying 'Look! I'm Superman!'" Phyllis laughed. "Who knew then?"

• • •

Plans had originally called for switching back and forth between the Kent farm and the dirt road, but Dick decided to wrap up the starship landing sequences before going back to the farm, a decision which pleased the exhausted crew. Naturally, though, on a film set, plans are made to be changed—or changed for you.

After the unit settled in to finish up on the Kent farm, the weather again turned bad—"We've never seen a summer like this! It's the worst August in forty-one years!," the Canadians kept assuring us—so Dick and Geoff Unsworth decided to do a lighting test in the large crystal starship back by the dirt road location.

When we had shifted again, Geoff expressed his concern that the green cellophane-covered lights inside the module might be too hot for little Aaron Smolinski, who played the baby Kal-El. And since I was the smallest person with the unit, I was hastily recruited to be Aaron's lighting double.

I had to strip down to the waist—it was no more than 55 degrees out, with a wet wind whipping across the vast expanse of wheat—and don a giant-size version of Aaron's costume, which rather resembled a diaper, all to the howls of the crew. Once I was inside the Lucite "crystal" module, filled with chirping crickets after having been left for two nights in the field, a fiendish David Tomblin mumbled for me to push open the hatch when Richard Hackman knocked on the back— and then David planted himself on top of the opening, trapping me in what seemed to be a 110-degree steam-bath as the lights went on, until my outcries made him relent.

When I finally did emerge, I was greeted by a roaring Dick Donner, along with Bob Penn and assorted other shutterbugs, madly filming away with their cameras. Bob said he would use the photo for the cover of *his* book about the seamy, behind-the-scenes life of a debauched American writer. And Dick threatened to keep the negatives under lock and key so that if I published anything objectionable about him, he could release them to the wire services with the story: "Perverted Unit Writer, Strung Out on Drugs, Spends Three Nights in the Space Capsule Committing Repeated Acts of Self-Abuse!"

•　　•　　•

The two days spent shooting baby Aaron emerging from the starship provided, surprisingly, a respite from the tension most people had been feeling, we had a chance to step back and smile, despite the difficulties.

Aaron was enchanting, coming out of the starship nude—as Dick finally decided—arms outstretched and a big grin on his face. It was a poignant moment; the intended allusion to Moses wasn't lost on any of us. I just wondered how the poor kid would live it down. I could imagine him twelve or fourteen years from now, at a local movie theater showing a re-release of an old movie entitled "Superman," and his date screaming "Oooo, Aaron! Is that *really* you?!?" much to his chagrin.

•　　•　　•

Finishing up on the starship, the production moved back once more to the Kent farm. The weather was now blustery and bitter cold (could it really be late August?) and the day proved to be a total washout. Most members of the unit were suffering from sore throats, Roy Button was down with aggravated high blood pressure (understandably), and poor Steve Barron was laid up with an abscessed tooth.

Also, as we neared the end of location work in North America (a sequence for "Superman II" at Niagara

Falls had mercifully been postponed), the air traffic controllers in England, like their comrades in Canada, were threatening a "go-by-the-book" slowdown over the upcoming three-day bank holiday weekend—the weekend we were scheduled to fly back to London. So Bob Simmonds in Calgary and Geoff Helman back at Pinewood started making alternative plans to reroute the worn-out unit via Toronto to either Amsterdam or Paris, and then by boat train to England. In all, a very depressing situation.

On top of that, the long-term weather forecast was very bad. That was it. The producers, gritting their teeth at the cost overruns, wanted to leave immediately. Dick Donner argued that they had to stay and try to complete needed scenes. Again fears were raised that the film might have to be compromised, fears of which Salkind and Spengler were only too painfully aware.

"Superman" was now weeks over schedule and millions over budget. The New York and Canadian locations had been anything but stunning successes. And the word from England wasn't really any better: the model units were way behind schedule and the flying unit was still encountering serious technical problems. A frantic Alexander Salkind was now on the transatlantic telephone almost every day, telling his son and Pierre Spengler that he could barely keep his bankers at bay.

The decision finally was made to complete only the scenes at the Kent farm with Phyllis and Jeff and leave the remaining shots to a Canadian second unit, with key personnel from the British crew to assist.

With that difficult decision behind him, though new forecasts predicted more rain, Donner decided to go ahead with a 4:30 A.M. call for the unit to try to get a sunrise shot on the Kent farm—the scene in which Clark Kent, after the death of his adoptive father, bids farewell to his "mother" and heads north, directed by some overpowering force.

It was cold and drizzling as we left the International Hotel, yawning, sighing, grumbling—many in the unit, in fact, hadn't bothered to go to sleep. After steaming cups of tea and the appropriate preparations of the setup, the crew stood staring at the horizon, trying to second-guess the experts as to where the sun would finally—if *ever*—break through the bank of clouds that had now begun to clear to the east.

Jeff East had been positioned in a wheat field off against the horizon, and Dick kept shifting him a few feet at a time, hoping to pick the spot where the sun would come up behind him. At last the clouds broke and turned to rose and gold. Peter MacDonald, crouching with his feet tucked under him, got it all down on film, to the joy and satisfaction of everyone, and we went on to shoot the scene in which young Clark and Ma Kent say goodbye for the last time.

We headed back to Calgary at midday. Immediately, everyone's thoughts turned toward England—home. The unit was scheduled to depart the next day.

Even with all the colds and sniffles, by now the only truly universal malady on the unit was homesickness. After several hard weeks on any film location, sooner or later everybody comes down with a bad case of it. It can be awfully lonely going back to a hotel room night after night.

"The telephone must be one of the most *insidious* inventions of the last hundred years," soundman Roy Charman observed, echoing the feelings of most of the married members of the crew, for whom the long separations become especially trying. "It doesn't just convey all the happy emotions, like the adverts try and convince you. It also intensifies the loneliness you feel when you're away. There's something terribly final when that receiver clicks down."

Certainly I related to this—it had happened to me, too. But I had very mixed emotions at the moment about going back to England. For me, it wasn't home. And the days ahead at Pinewood were not going to be easy.

Location had largely been a story of delays and spiraling costs. And much of the most difficult and crucial work, the special effects, was still to be done in the eight remaining weeks scheduled for shooting at the studio.

It looked, however, as if the most challenging special effect would be delivering the picture on time.

9
Super sets—Super setbacks

For Dick Donner and most of the rest of the crew, settling back in at Pinewood meant getting through a mountainous backlog of work, not only what had been accomplished at the studio in the months that the main unit had been gone, but also the eight weeks' worth of location filming that Stuart Baird and his editorial staff were already hard at work on. Some of the footage coming back from North America was of questionable quality. "We had problems in New York," Peter MacDonald told me. "When you shoot wide open, in variable light, there is very little depth of focus. So you have to be right on . . . you're either sharp or you're soft. Unfortunately, we had a good deal of it soft. Some of it should have been soft, mind you, but maybe not quite as much as there was."

On top of that was the breakneck shooting schedule everyone had to face. Fortunately, Richard Lester, in his one major decision affecting the film, recommended that all efforts be concentrated on finishing "Superman I"—"Superman II" could be reactivated later. Donner and the producers enthusiastically agreed.

Soon after getting back to Pinewood, I talked to Chris Reeve about his first summer as Superman. We spoke in his dressing room and he was in costume, looking even huskier than he had just six weeks ago in New York—perhaps it was the natty red cape.

Did he still bristle, I asked, when the media referred to him as an "unknown"?

"Well, it's a relative term." Chris smiled. "There is a difference between 'unknown' and 'inexperienced.' I may well be unknown, but some people, the hard core of soap opera addicts, would know who I am"—Reeve played young Ben Harper on "Love of Life" for several seasons—"though perhaps nobody else. But I'm *not* inexperienced. I started in the theater when I was fifteen and joined Equity when I was sixteen. After performing with a theater group, I was hired by a repertory company in Boston to act in 'The Games,' 'A Month in the Country,' 'Death of a Salesman' and 'The Hostage.' After that summer, I went back to high school in Princeton where I'd grown up; I had a very good arrangement with the headmaster of the high school, by which I was allowed to cut out for matinees and that sort of thing. And I worked at the McArthur Theater Company—a professional repertory like the Arena in Washington, D.C.—where I played the kid in 'Our Town,' I also did 'Much Ado About Nothing.'"

Chris stopped to take a call from David Tomblin, who told him that preparations for the flying setups on "A" stage would take at least another twenty minutes. Then he went on: "In college, I got an agent and I really started. I used to come down from Cornell, cut classes for a day and make appointments for films and TV. And then I'd go back and make up the homework. So I did the occasional television spot while I was still at college. My senior year at Cornell, I was one of three people admitted to the advanced program at the Juilliard School for Drama. Juilliard used to be exclusively for music, but they introduced drama in 1968. So my senior year at college and my advance year at Juilliard were simultaneous. I graduated from Cornell—B.A. in literature—but I had to study another year at Juilliard. It was like having a year abroad, that kind of thing. And I did everything, mind you—a great deal of training. I finally did some voice work, some ballet, fencing, stage fighting, acrobatics, circus, mime—all of it. And then that summer, I went back to Boston and got a part in 'Threepenny Opera.'

"Just after that I was hired to play Ben on 'Love of Life.' It was a bit complicated, because I had only taken that job to pay for my second year at Juilliard, and then they decided they needed the character more than they had expected. It was supposed to be one or two days a week, but they said, 'Now that the character is doing so well, we're going to need you four or five times a week.' So I had to quit Juilliard and I ended up being on television for those two years, during which I tried to get plays as often as possible. I worked with the Circle Repertory Company, and with the Manhattan Theater Club. Then I played opposite Katharine Hepburn in the Enid Bagnold play, 'A Matter of Gravity,' on Broadway—all while I was still doing the soap opera. People ask me *now*, 'When were you so skinny. When were you this 'toothpick kid' we've heard so much publicity about?'" Chris grinned. "I was really in poor shape back then."

Looking at his strapping muscular physique, I found that hard to believe.

"I was down to a hundred eighty pounds and was absolutely a wreck! I looked ashen, you know, really bad, because I was riding the rails between Toronto or Washington or some place like that, and I would have to get out at four in the morning to take a plane to New York, learning the lines on the plane since I had to be at CBS by seven-thirty to do a full day's work on the soap till five in the evening. Then I'd hop another plane at six, shuttle back to Washington or wherever and be on stage at eight. That was twice a week for sixteen weeks. Since then, it's been more plays, a small film part—and now this.

"So I *do* bristle when I'm called inexperienced, because I put in my time."

All the same, I observed, landing a role like Superman must have made him feel that he had made a big step toward acting success.

"If you were to ask me 'What do you want out of this film?' I would say that what I really want is for it to have been a smart decision—in terms of *acting*. That I didn't sell myself short. Success comes only if you experience it that way, at least for me. For instance, people said to me, 'Oh . . . you're playing the leading man opposite Katharine Hepburn! My God! What a *success!*' But the play wasn't very good, the production was weak, and it wasn't a success in my terms because the play didn't come alive until its second tour. Just to *be* someplace is not success. It's what you make of it . . . how you use it. It's a very relative term. I see it all in terms of building—step by step by step. As long as you keep climbing the ladder and improving your talent, setting new targets for yourself, that's success. But suddenly to be billed the headliner in a movie— that's not necessarily success. You could disappear tomorrow."

I asked Chris how his family and friends had reacted to his new role during his brief visit to New York and New Jersey in July.

"My father missed the boat completely!" Reeve grinned again. "When I first got the part and told him, he thought I was going to be in a movie of Bernard Shaw's 'Man and Superman'! I remember, I was doing a play on Broadway and one night after the show I told him 'I've got Superman!' and he said, 'Fantastic!' —you know, the whole works, champagne on the table and everything. Then I said, 'Perhaps I ought to tell you, it's not *that* Superman. It's the one who flies through the air like in the comic book. . . .' 'Oh,' said my father. So that brought him down a little bit. I guess I can understand that from someone who teaches Russian literature."

Chris became more serious. "My family have been

—151—

through a lot of changes. They know it's not like I've been sold up the Amazon River into captivity and I'll never be seen again or something. The automatic assumption that's usually made is: 'Oh well, he's going to be in a big movie and he'll change his phone number' —yes, I may well change my phone number!—'so now we can't talk to him. Now he's going to have a secretary, you know, to answer his phone and stuff like that.' Well, that's crazy! I mean, I treat this movie in the same way as I would treat being in a Broadway play. It simply boils down to how you do the work.

"So when my family and relatives and friends understood that I was working on this the same as I'd work on anything else, then they all relaxed about it. There's the occasional odd comment, you know, from my father —who's a novelist and poet and Russian scholar. And my mother . . . well, my mother, I can't tell her anything about the movie without some risk: she's a newspaper reporter! She'll call me and say, 'We haven't heard from you in a while,' and I'll say, 'Well, mom, I've been pretty busy,' and she'll say, 'Well, whatever it is, make sure we get the story before the other papers do!' So we have these little arguments now and then, and I say, 'Be a relative! You're *my mother*, not just a newspaper reporter. Let other people write the story.' "

•   •   •

Principal photography resumed on "E" stage with some last crucial scenes from "Superman II" before the new moratorium on the sequel took effect—it was essential to finish scenes from parts I *and* II involving super-salaried stars like Brando and Hackman.

One of these sequences dealt with a daring aerial escape in a balloon by Lex Luthor and Miss Teschmacher. Hackman and Perrine were in a big wicker basket, dangling by rope and cable from the top of the stage, and all the action was photographed against a giant blue screen as a traveling matte shot.

Since many scenes in "Superman" required this specialized type of filming, it's worth a brief explanation.

The traveling matte is today's sophisticated equivalent of the old "process shot," in which characters were filmed in front of an often unconvincing scene projected on a screen behind them. For the balloon sequence, a location camera crew shot exterior footage, while the foreground scenes were shot on "E" stage in front of the blue screen. The overall blue tone of the foreground film allows it to be integrated perfectly with the background, with no telltale flickering edges, when the two are blended in an optical printer.

•   •   •

Valerie Perrine had taken the Concorde from Washington after participating in Ethel Kennedy's celebrity tennis tournament at Forest Hills, New York, and she flitted around the set telling everyone that her doubles partner had been Ilie Nastase and that she had beaten actress Dina Merrill in singles.

At lunchtime on the first full shooting day back at the studio, I saw some rushes of the incredibly beautiful sunrise scenes that had been filmed at the Kent farm in Blackie.

Later, on the flying stage, I found that while we had been on location the flying unit had come up with yet another innovation: a midget, wearing a tiny wig, a latex Chris Reeve mask and pint-sized Superman suit, was being used as a double for Chris in some of the long shots.

After finishing the process work with Perrine and Hackman, the main unit shifted to "D" stage and one of the most fantastic sets in the entire production. In fact, it edged out the colossal Fortress of Solitude as my personal favorite.

John Barry had designed Luthor's lair, a subterranean hideaway deep within the bowels of an abandoned section of Grand Central Station in Metropolis. As the screenplay describes it: "Luthor's Lair is palatial. At first glance, it is breathtaking with its multi-leveled areas, only some of which are immediately visible. A massive desk sits off to one side. Behind it, the entire wall which rises to a high ceiling is covered with full bookcases bulging with periodicals, papers, etc. Another separate area has complicated banks of electronic gadgets which have been connected to underground electrical lines exposed in portions of the rock-faced walls. In the same way we discover exposed heating ducts and water mains. (There is a 'pit' area near LUTHOR's desk which presumably sinks down to a much lower level and is occupied by various unseen monsters whose vicious growls and snarls occasionally punctuate the scene. Visible claw marks line the back wall of the pit.)"

Looking at all the imaginative and inspired effort that had gone into Luthor's lair, it was easy for me to understand how Barry and his team had won the Academy Award for "Star Wars."

The massive set had five major divisions: a sundeck-patio area, complete with palm trees, chaise longues, umbrellas, sand and, for "sun," assorted ultraviolet lamps; a study, with appropriate clutter, serving as Luthor's office; a major and minor set of control rooms, with computer banks, blinking light panels, dials, and sinister-looking "black boxes"; and, as the focal point of the whole set, an indoor swimming pool at the foot of an old, blocked-off marble staircase.

The extra touches were magnificent—cobwebs, which had to be continually retouched, covering the massive brass chandelier (flawlessly reproduced in polystyrene) as well as the enormous statue overhanging the pool area. There was also a huge crumbling board listing long-ago train arrivals and departures, assorted crumbling marble banisters made of "marble-ized" plaster (a painstaking process still done by hand in the Pinewood shops), reams of papers and old books, and assorted toys and playthings, including old-fashioned pinball machines and a filmed backdrop of the Caribbean projected onto three screens behind the makeshift "beach."

Surveying the lair before the unit had actually moved over from "E" stage, Geoff Unsworth dryly said, "It'll look all right when I've lit it!"

The actors and crew appeared to enjoy working on the Luthor's lair set, even though the intricate multi-level design didn't do much to speed up the shooting.

Between takes Valerie and Gene Hackman chatted and joked with the crew, often providing us with some memorable off-camera entertainment. I asked Gene if I could shove him into the pool—it would have made a super still for the book—but he just gave me a very strange look. Occasionally, when a few reporters were allowed on the stage, I would ask Val if she was free for an interview. "I'm *never* free, darlin', but my price is going down every day!" she'd reply.

• • •

By now eight film units were at work on "Superman." At Pinewood were the main unit, a second unit, plus flying, model and two matte units; another unit was shooting in Canada; and there was a plate unit in New York City. By early '78, the total would be even higher. The more people working on the production (at its height, over 1,000), the more it seemed to expand, as if in a conscious effort to make it bigger and better than anything that had gone before. If a flying shot looked hokey or an effects sequence wasn't 100 percent perfect,

Dick would toss it out and schedule a reshoot. Soon the word was going around the lot: the film was being retitled "Superman—Super Retake."

I began to divide my time between the main unit and the effects units.

Derek Meddings and his expert model team were busy shooting a highly complex sequence in which Air Force One is struck by lightning in a sudden freak thunderstorm. They were working with an exact scaleddown replica of the famous aircraft—complete with tiny flashing red lights, a fully lit interior cabin and the familiar Presidential seal on the side of the nose. As the little plane tumbled and turned on wires and hydraulic armatures through unseen turbulence, Paul Wilson, the cameraman, gave periodic shouts for artificial lightning, to create just the right effect.

The second unit, meanwhile, was at work on shots of a yellow school bus, specially shipped in from the States, which is caught on the Golden Gate Bridge in the midst of the massive earthquake induced by Lex Luthor. They would also shoot a scene (later scrubbed from the film) in which a Girl Scout troop is rescued by Superman from the quake.

There was even night shooting going on, with further scenes from the helicopter sequence in Metropolis (already shot in New York) being filmed on a two-story mock-up of the top of the *Daily Planet* building, as well as retakes of shots which Donner didn't entirely like. (Dick panicked at rushes because he was sure the pontoons on the mock-up helicopter were the wrong color. He was right.)

The main unit was making preparations for the scene in which Superman, with a chunk of lethal green kryptonite chained around him, is pushed into the pool by the fiendish Lex Luthor. I chatted with John Barry and people from the art and property departments about the highly specialized items that had been designed for Luthor's lair—like the special newspapers with headlines that read "CAPED WONDER SAVES THE CITY" above pictures of Chris Reeve as Superman; film tapes for internal TV sets in Lex's computer rooms, special maps showing Luthor's plans for what would be the West Coast after the destruction of California, complete with names like "Lex Springs," "Marina del Lex," "Otisland" (instead of Disneyland?) and the like.

Peter Howitt's set dressing for Luthor's lair was particularly extravagant, with classic French phones, crystal obelisks, rare (or at least old) books, and an assortment of oddities which looked like a Portobello Road jumble sale. I remember particularly a fantastic-looking antique inkwell in the shape of a reclining devil, knees bent and legs spread apart, with a cauldron—which served as the actual well—set between them. It even had a writhing sinner—perhaps a bad *writer*—struggling to get out.

While they were shooting the scene in which Superman opens the lead chest containing the fragment of kryptonite, Chris got a ribbing from Gene Hackman. On the first take, Chris, unaware of his own now well-developed strength, threw back the lid so violently that the chest was knocked off its platform. Just as Dick yelled "Cut!", Gene sheepishly repeated his line, "I told you not to open it!, and everyone cracked up. And just before the last take, Gene had the lid nailed down, so that when Chris delivered his line, "I'll bend this box into your prison bars, Luthor!" and stooped to snap back the lid, he got quite a surprise—if not a hernia!

At rushes the next day, there was a lovely look at a scene during which Chris had stepped on one of Gene's lines, inspiring a smiling Hackman, sitting in the theater, to say, "See, first *you* talk, then *I* talk, then *you* talk, then *I* talk. . . ."

Val Perrine was having her own technical difficulties. Apparently Dick had been voicing concern that most of her costumes were making a too-prominent display of her nipples. And indeed, Perrine's nipples were undeniably evident. A solution was found when one of the wardrobe mistresses inserted elastoplast to round the breasts off.

That wasn't the only problem poor Valerie was having with her chest. During a shot in the lair, in which she had to run into Luthor's study, she complained to Dick that her breasts bounced too much. Not to worry, Dick soothed her—Peter MacDonald would be sure to follow them with a bouncing camera movement!

A climactic scene in the film is Superman's fall into the swimming pool with the deadly green-glowing chunk of kryptonite.

The day they began to shoot this scene, Geoff Unsworth had to keep assuring a concerned Dick Donner that the battery-operated kryptonite was completely sealed and waterproof, preventing anyone from receiving a nasty shock.

Hackman shoved Chris with the kryptonite into the pool, and Dick got several shots of him floundering and thrashing before going under. Now it was time for a somewhat reformed Miss Teschmacher to come to the rescue. But Valerie wasn't in particularly good form when it came time for her plunge into the pool. Dick kept shouting that her delivery wasn't convincing; she banged her knee on the underwater stairs; she even forgot to put in her contact lenses (tinted almost royal blue), and had to send a Steve Lanning scurrying back to her make-up box, from which he returned to inform the actress that both her lens cases appeared to be labeled "Right eye."

And then came the scene in which Miss Teschmacher, before rescuing the hapless Man of Steel, steals a kiss. Despite several rehearsals, it looked more like an X-rated loop than a quick peck in a family film. (Dick kept screaming at Perrine: "I want a *short, simple, high-school kiss!*") And after each take, Chris had to jump out of the water, have a new battery pack attached— when Miss Teschmacher ripped the chain off him, it pulled out the connecting wires—and be recombed and made up for the next shot.

In the end, the shot looked marvelous. And certainly no one could have questioned Val's effort and enthusiasm. After the final take, she emerged from the pool with about six huge rips under the arms of her thousand-dollar white chiffon dress.

The next morning, John Williams, the Academy Award-winning composer of the scores for such box-office blockbusters as "The Towering Inferno," "Jaws," "Star Wars," and "Close Encounters of the Third Kind," arrived on the set to meet with Dick Donner. (The Salkinds had just formally announced the signing of Williams, unquestionably Hollywood's hottest music man. His "Star Wars" record album had already grossed an amazing $20 million, more than most films do!).

The last two days on Luthor's lair, the unit had to shoot several scenes in the small interior control room, making use of the VTRs—videotape recorders—hooked into six television monitors scattered around the room, all of which made for intricate, slow-moving work. As with the earlier sequence with Brando and the three Krypton super-villains, cameraman Peter MacDonald was having a great deal of difficulty with the film projections. The problem was interlocking his camera and the VTRs at the proper speed to prevent "flutter" or other telltale imperfections.

"When you're working like this," MacDonald told me, "having everything coordinated at the correct speed is crucial. Take the flying shots, for example—of paramount importance. Now, we know Superman flies 'faster than a speeding bullet.' But as the script indicates, sometimes he takes off leisurely, sometimes he lolls around in the sky, other times he's rocketing through space faster than the speed of light. It's our job to make it all look believable. The standard camera speed is twenty-four frames per second. If you slow the camera down to twenty frames per second, that speeds the action up, because you're compressing more action into fewer frames. Conversely, if you increase the camera speed to thirty frames per second, you slow the action down, since less action is being spread over more frames. So according to what's called for in a particular sequence, everything has to be figured right on the mark."

To break the tension after they wrapped on "D" stage, David Tomblin and Donner arranged a birthday party on the set for a.d. Steve Lanning. After the birthday cake and champagne, Valerie and Gene emerged from their dressing rooms in terrycloth robes, suddenly stood shoulder-to-shoulder, turned, bent over, lifted their robes and "mooned" the entire crew! (I tried to get a still of that memorable happening so that I could caption it "Is this *the end* of Superman?" but no such luck.)

•   •   •

That weekend, Christopher Reeve celebrated his twenty-fifth birthday—"If we can just perfect the flying before Chris applies for Medicare," one senior production official sighed—and on Monday morning, the main unit moved over to the gigantic 007 stage to begin work on Superman's mighty Fortress of Solitude.

John Barry's set, on which construction had started back in June, was nothing short of breathtaking. Filling the entire 374' by 160' by 53' stage, it was a phantasmagoric representation of the North Pole, complete with towering glaciers and jagged ice peaks. At one end, as if about to pierce the sky, was Barry's crystalline interpretation of the exterior of the enormous Fortress of Solitude itself.

To create a sparkling, reflective, snowbound effect, the entire stage had been covered with the contents of hundreds of 50-kilogram (110-pound) bags of dendritic dairy salt. The cost of the salt alone, Barry informed me, had been a whopping six thousand dollars.

The cavernus submarine tank, seen in "The Spy Who Loved Me," had been filled with water on which floated huge styrofoam-and-plywood glaciers and ice floes.

The stage was totally surrounded by a *hand-painted* sky backdrop, complete with aurora borealis, over which Geoff Unsworth had hung a gauze netting to diffuse the lighting, for which sixteen generator trucks had been brought in.

To add to the convincing feeling of a vast frozen wasteland, a cold haze, created by fog machines and mountains of dry ice, hung over the set, giving the Fortress an appropriately eerie atmosphere.

Because of the water, the corrosive salt, the dry ice and other hazards, most of the crew were issued knee-high Wellington boots, and some of the special-effects and construction crew had to don full rubber wetsuits for work in the tank. Extra care had to be taken with all the camera, sound and lighting equipment too, to make sure none of the potentially destructive salt stayed on overnight. And by now, well into autumn, the weather in England had again turned chilly; in the vast aluminum-sided stage, the temperature on a windy day was just above 50 degrees.

For the first few days on the Fortress set, nobody seemed to mind the adversities; between takes or at tea breaks, the crew would sit on the snow-cats and other Arctic rescue equipment and sing "Walking in a Winter Wonderland" or "Jingle Bells."

Unfortunately, that mood didn't prevail for long, as night after night David Tomblin was forced to ask the crew for the quarter, half hour or hour in overtime needed to complete the day's shooting. And Valerie Perrine and Gene Hackman, wearing their heavy fur costumes, hot even on the cold set, became increasingly irritable as they neared the end of their stints on the film.

One of the few people who seemed to remain unflappable was Geoff Unsworth, always the perfect gentleman, always quick with a smile and usually quick with a solution to any lighting problem. "The bigger the challenge, the more I like the job," said the man who lit "2001: A Space Odyssey" and "Cabaret," for which he won an Oscar, "and this is surely just about the most demanding film I've ever worked on."

The main challenge facing Dick Donner now was how to be in ten different places at once. The director had to shuttle among main-unit shooting (of scenes from both "Superman" I and II) with Hackman and Perrine, the second-unit filming with Ned Beatty on "D" stage, Chris and the flying unit on "A" stage, and the two model and matte units. (Dick wisely had the production office lease him a golf cart so that he could cover the studio grounds faster.)

One particularly tense day on the 007 stage, as everyone anxiously awaited Dick's return from one of the other units, an impatient Gene Hackman, swathed in his bulky furs under the hot lights, suddenly threw down a key prop, Colin Chilver's carefully constructed "black box," smashing it to bits and further delaying shooting until quick repairs had been made.

Just as spirits were reaching a new low—there was even the possibility of a walkout of Pinewood employees who wanted additional hardship pay because of the adverse conditions on the Fortress set—a note on the call sheets announced that there would be a screening in Theater #7 of a thirty-minute "Superman" promotional reel that had been assembled primarily for the benefit of the Warner Brothers brass. For most of the crew members, this would be a first look at footage from the extraordinary movie they had been laboring on for more than seven months.

The screening was a tonic, far beyond what the producers or Dick could have expected. Scenes of the fantastic planet Krypton, of Jor-El and Lara bidding farewell to their infant son, of the awesome destruction of the planet, of the windswept wheat fields, of the fast-paced beat of the *Daily Planet* city room and, finally, of Superman streaking through the air, brought foot-stamping, hand-clapping cheers of approval.

The reaction confirmed what was in everyone's mind: they were onto a winner.

•   •   •

Gene Hackman finished up on "Superman" without many farewells; he seemed anxious to get back to Los Angeles. Valerie's final scene on the film involved night work, and she spent most of the last evening moping on the wet, cold set, sipping champagne between takes. Ned Beatty, who also completed his role with night work, made careful rounds, saying goodbye to various crew members and thanking everyone for helping him enjoy his first visit overseas.

The day after the three principals had departed, I climbed to the top of the 007 stage to get a better perspective of the massive set. About halfway up the iron ladder, I froze, an instant victim of acrophobia. I finally inched my way to the top and made my way gingerly along the catwalk, introducing myself to the puzzled-looking riggers and electricians. "Hi, I'm writing the book about the filming of 'Superman,'" I told them shakily, trying to forget where I was. They thought I was a nut case!

•   •   •

Night work was still continuing on the helicopter sequence—new scenes had also been shot at nearby Luton Airport—and most drizzly evenings, the crew could be found hovering around one of the camera vans, where second-unit clapper-loader Nick Schlesinger would usually be making strong coffee or grilling sausages on a tiny stove. Often it seemed as if they had to spend more time waiting for the weather to clear than actually shooting. Despite lots of eating, *exterior* filming in England is never a picnic.

During the waiting one evening, I persuaded Colin Chilvers, who was responsible for most of the outlandish mechanical effects on the Ken Russell films "Tommy" and "Lisztomania," to demonstrate the mock-up helicopter. It was mainly of plywood (except for the rear section, which came from an actual helicopter that had crashed near the studios), and the entire mock-up was attached to a massive hydraulic armature, which could make it pitch, roll, swoop, and dive convincingly. Since the 'copter would be largely destroyed by the end of shooting, Colin explained, using the real thing, as in New York, would cost too much—about $300,000.

Later I wandered past the dressing rooms, where I mischievously ripped Gene Hackman's name off his door. I stuck it that night on the door of my hotel room, just to see if I'd get any reactions. There was a litter of notes from hotel guests under the door the next morning, though I found it hard to imagine anyone believing that Hackman would actually advertise where he was. A sampling: "Gene, we think you're great" and "Gene, we loved your last movie." My favorite said, quite directly, "Gene . . . give me a call at Mutchie's Bar, South Street, N.Y.C. 10020 when you get back."

•   •   •

While the main unit on the 007 stage was shooting a scene in which Jeff East as the young Clark Kent tosses a crystal from Jor-El into the frigid waters, thus creating the crystalline Fortress, at the other end of the stage Dick Donner was struggling to get flying shots of the three super-villains, Ursa, Non and General Zod, soaring over the Fortress. These shots were for the now-shelved "Superman II," but because they involved Terence Stamp, Sarah Douglas and Jack O'Halloran, Dick wanted to get them in the can, rather than recall the trio in the future.

As with all the flying work on the film, these scenes were incredibly tedious to set up. There was one bad moment when big Jack O'Halloran, a former heavyweight boxer, was inadvertently left dangling in midair for ten uncomfortable minutes while Dick, David Tomblin and others huddled over some new problem. "Get me the hell down from here!" O'Halloran boomed suddenly at the startled men below. As they hauled him in backwards, Jack was screaming, "Who built this goddam thing, anyway?"

Following that incident, I left the 007 stage for the quieter but only slightly less chaotic atmosphere of the model unit, busy on F stage filming a scaled-down version of the entire planet Krypton with an impressive new camera technique.

The "Louma," an acronym of the names of its two French inventors, Jean-Pierre Lavalou and Alain Messeron, is a unique camera device which can make a complete 360-degree vertical loop while filming, thereby opening up a while new realm of possibilities for impressive tracking shots—just what was needed for the sweeping, wide angle perspective of the stark, white crystalline exterior of the mysterious planet.

* * *

At the end of October, with months of scheduled shooting yet to go, most of the main unit suddenly received their two-week notices. Rumors flew faster than Superman: the producers were bankrupt; Warner Brothers had seized the film; Donner had been fired; the budget had been drastically slashed and the film would be put together from footage already shot.

Of course, no single story was true, but elements of some of them had basis in reality. The original shooting schedule, perhaps the greatest fantasy of the film, had called for an end to principal photography by the last week of October. As the deadline approached and the delivery date for the film loomed, the producers hoped to give the impression to the outside world—including the distributors—that most of the film had been finished, and that only special-effects work remained. The mass dismissal was also a way for Alexander Salkind to try to stem the skyrocketing budget and convince his financial backers that everything was under control. There were other pieces to the puzzle which few people knew about, but obviously a major power struggle was going on.

Most crew members who received notice seemed elated to have the end in sight for this long, difficult and often unhappy production.

Invitations went out reading: "Alexander Salkind, Richard Donner, Ilya Salkind, Pierre Spengler and Richard Lester cordially invite you to an end of production reception on Friday, 28th of October, at 6:15 P.M. until 8:30 P.M. in the Green Room at Pinewood Studios." " 'End of production'—that's just the production office's euphemism for 'We've gotta cut costs, boys,' " a key crew member said sardonically.

With time running out fast, main-unit shooting continued on a new set, Lois Lane's terrace, on "M" stage. What had already been shot for the terrace scene in New York was soft-focus and displeased Donner on a number of counts, so the director had ordered new footage along with the crucial additional scenes that had already been scheduled.

The set for Lois's terrace was large and lavish, a bit much for the apartment of a Metropolis working girl, I thought; a rooftop pad like that in New York would rent for more than a thousand a month. Surrounded by backlit cutouts of Metropolis skyscrapers, as well as huge silver screens for the complex front-projection shots, the terrace set consisted of a sizeable flagstone patio by redwood walkways and filled with hundreds of varieties of plants. The terrace opened off a large foyer, to one side of which was Lois's bedroom.

As usual, just when shooting was to begin, Dick, Geoff Unsworth, Peter MacDonald and a half dozen other people decided that alterations had to be made: an awning over the French doors was too low and had to be cut free to be readjusted; the "brick" around the terrace had to be rebuilt in sections—and on and on and on.

In the evening, just after wrapping, there was a tearful argument between Margot Kidder and the costume department. She had wanted to wear her own clothes all along, she protested; she prevailed—and a thousand-dollar dress had to be discarded.

A happier mood prevailed on the set the next day, with Donner playfully calling Chris "Soupy" and Margot "Irving." (She, in turn, gave the director the pet name of "Harry.") During one rehearsal, Margot doused herself in wine, thinking the glass she held was empty, and then, moments later, drew howls from the crew in a sequence in which Lois in interviewing Superman: "Now, what about your vital parts? Superman, how *big* are you?" Then a moment's silence before the gales of laughter. "Ooops . . . I meant: how *tall* . . . how *tall* are you?!"

Later in the week, Gary Kurtz, the young producer of "Star Wars," paid a visit to the set, talking with many of the crew members who had worked on his box-office bonanza. Kurtz had also stopped by the shooting while the picture was on location in Canada, and met with Ilya and Pierre. Now, with this second visit, there was considerable speculation that Kurtz was being enticed to bail the production out. In fact, he was there to start lining up crew for "Star Wars II."

In addition to Kurtz that week, there were also visitors representing Eastern European film production (much of it government controlled) who, even behind the Iron Curtain, had heard the ballyhoo about the mammoth "Superman" enterprise. And one of Charlie Chaplin's young daughters, who knew several of the crew from "A Bridge Too Far," came to have her photograph taken with Christopher Reeve.

Chris seemed pleased to have an excuse to leave the set momentarily between takes—and with good reason. The excessively hot lights had brought back an old problem, and Yvonne Blake had to assign wardrobe staffers to dry Chris's sweat-soaked costume with portable hair blowers before each shot.

The first of the allegedly final two weeks ended with Model Unit 1's destruction of Krypton back on "F" stage.

The set—a layered, jigsaw-style construction of painted white plywood and greenish-tinted plastics—had been rigged and wired with explosives and blasting caps, including the enormous two-story section that contained Jor-El's laboratory. The arc lights overhead had been covered in red cellophane to bathe the stage in a fiery red glow. Smoke machines filled the area with thick white smoke. After each "stop action" shot, an original section of the set was replaced by a partially destroyed one in preparation for the final explosion—the huge dome over the council chamber was replaced with a melted, crushed one, and two-, three-, and four-foot charred replicas of the pulsing columns of light in Jor-El's lab were substituted for the gleaming chrome-like ones.

Finally, at 6:00 P.M., the blue and red lights over the stage flashed and crackled lightning, the wired charges exploded, a barrage of metal from an air gun (usually employed to shoot "blood" pellets in a gunfight scene) riddled the set, sending dust and splinters flying; and then suddenly, the whole central breakaway went crashing down in a heap of rubble, producing a round of applause from the obviously satisfied unit.

All of that "magic," as the model unit liked to call its effects, cost a great deal of money, as did everything else on the film. Production accountant Douggie Noakes explained why "Superman" was fast becoming a financial landmark in the annals of motion-picture production. Flipping through the massive ledgers which littered his office, Noakes told me that on any given week the accounts office processed an average of two hundred invoices. This particular week, an unusually heavy one, they had totaled a staggering half million dollars! By this point in the shooting, the accounts office had processed over five thousand invoices. Petty cash flowed freely too, with the weekly average hovering between $30 and $40 thousand—a helluva lot of paper clips and cab fares!

•   •   •

Since the "end of principal photography" was supposedly approaching, activity on the production was nothing short of amazing.

Though shooting on Lois's terrace was incomplete, Dick had ordered the set struck—it would have to be rebuilt later—since they were two weeks over schedule on it and the studio had been forced to reclaim the stage for another production.

So the main unit moved back to the 007 stage; the second unit shifted to the North Tunnel "diner" set for another needed sequence from "Superman II"; the flying unit continued filming the helicopter crash; the model unit started shooting the Golden Gate Bridge on the back lot. And Dick Donner scurried back and forth among all the units in an effort to be everywhere at once. "It's almost impossible to coordinate this film," Geoff Unsworth sighed in sympathy.

On the Fortress of Solitude set, Donner was still filming the scene of Jeff East creating the Fortress with
Jor-El's crystal. "It looks like an electric cucumber,"
jibed one of the camera crew. "More like a fluorescent
dildo," retorted one of the a.d.'s. "That's all that's left of
the Jolly Green Giant," joked one of the plasterers,
glancing skeptically at the pulsing green plastic rod.

There were also preliminaries for a scene with a polar
bear, fashioned by master make-up artist Stu Freeborn,
and for a long-distance shot of foot-high "G.I. Joe"-type
dolls doubling for Arctic patrol corpsmen.

In preparation for the polar bear shot, a fantastically
realistic remote-controlled miniature of an amphibious
Arctic sled, complete with tiny costumed dolls doubling
for Gene Hackman and Valerie Perrine, was placed far
off in the tank. Then, at the other end, wet-suited divers,
wearing masks, flippers and oxygen tanks, lowered Freeborn's expertly crafted polar bear into the water so that
one of the divers could position himself inside the upper
portion. Dick instructed him to make slow, paddling
motions with the front paws. Unfortunately, it looked
more as though the paws were attached to paddle
wheels and no matter how many adjustments were
made, Dick was dissatisfied with the look of the bear in
the water. By the time they pulled it out late in the
afternoon, dripping wet and covered with salt "snow,"
the bear seemed to be afflicted with terminal mange.

The next day of shooting, the last before the supposed "end of production," saw most of the departing
crew bidding each other farewell, though the main unit
spent much of the day completing matte work on the
007 stage.

On all "long haul" productions, there is almost always
a great deal of personnel turnover, as people move on
to new productions that offer fresh challenges—or, at
least, several months of what they hope will be steady
employment. In this respect, "Superman" was like other

films, and though Dick and the production office may have worried about continuity of style and preserving the high standards of the film, this was only the first of many "changings of the guard."

•   •   •

It was a glorious, warm, Indian-summer day for the "wrap" party, and the same lighthearted and convivial mood that had characterized the set in the last several days was still evident.

The producers and their invaluable assistant Maria Monreal had been making plans for the fête for a good ten days, but for some reason not all the invitations went out at the same time and a general reminder about the party hadn't appeared until the previous day's call sheet, which led to some grumblings that the party was a last-minute afterthought.

The party itself more than made up for any lapses in protocol. The entire Green Room (part of the Pinewood restaurant complex) had been lavishly decorated with Superman paraphernalia and floral arrangements, including two enormous Superman emblems in red and yellow carnations. There was a big open bar, cases of champagne, a generous buffet—fried chicken, sausage rolls, hamburgers, hot dogs, shrimp, salads. For dessert: two huge Superman cakes. A band provided music and a disco had been set up opposite the bar.

In addition to cast and crew, the producers had invited many of their fellow filmmakers based at Pinewood, as well as several business and financial associates and many celebrities from the London entertainment scene. Christopher Reeve made his way through the mob, smiling, chatting, shaking hands, looking relaxed in desert boots, jeans and an open white shirt with the sleeves rolled up. Margot, dressed in her own interpretation of punk, with black velvet bow tie, gray vest and jacket, boogied joyfully with members of the crew.

The party was supposed to be over by 8:30, but when I left, soon after nine, people seemed just to be getting started—laughing, eating, kissing, getting drunk. In the garden, you could hear the retching noises reminiscent of the scene outside pubs after closing on a Saturday night. One poor fellow staggered through the glass French doors of a gazebo built for "The Great Gatsby," but was more dazed than hurt. The studio gatekeeper told me the next morning that at 6:30 A.M., the gardens surrounding the Green Room had "looked more like Victoria Station at rush hour than Pinewood."

The consensus was that it had been one of the best wrap parties ever.

10
Putting on the writs

After a brief trip to the States, I returned to Pinewood
in mid-November to find that principal photography on
"Superman" was still halted and that most key people
were on leave. Dick Donner was back in L.A., Geoff
Unsworth was taking a brief holiday in England, Pierre
Spengler was in meetings with Alex in Paris, and Ilya
was in New York checking on the promotion, publicity
and merchandising campaigns of the rapidly expanding
"Superman" empire.

Chris Reeve was available, though, and I asked him
one afternoon at the studio if the enormously commercial aspects of the film posed any problems for a serious
actor like himself.

"Well, at first . . . yes," Chris admitted. "At first when
they said, " 'Do you want to go up for the lead in
"Superman"?' I laughed. I thought I was a ridiculous
possibility for Superman, weighing about one hundred
eighty-eight pounds or whatever. But I always take a
reading, whatever it is. I mean, if they ask me to go up
for the lead role in *The Joy of Cooking*, you know, I'll
take a reading on it, just to find out what it's about.
Even though later I'll say, 'My God, they wanted me
to play the egg part!' "

Chris paused for a moment, his brow furrowed. "But
at first I thought, 'Oh, Jesus, who needs this. This is
going to be a multimillion-dollar disaster, this is 'King

Kong.' Why can't Hollywood learn to do something decent, do intelligent, new scripts!' Then I got the script and found it *was* an intelligent, new script. They also had Brando and Hackman, Trevor Howard and Terry Stamp, and Mario Puzo wrote the screenplay, and I thought, 'This is not a joke!' When I saw how it was going to be done, I thought, 'I'm gonna just play it *my* way.' I treated the screen test as if it were a scene rehearsal for an acting class. And in acting class, they don't care who the hell you are! You just come in and show them your work. So I did the test for Clark Kent the way I wanted, with the stammer, the slouch, mannerisms I sort of invented myself. And what I put in was accepted. In no way was I treated like, you know, 'Here's the hunk off the beach; put him in the blue costume and stand him over there.' Sure, Brando's in the movie, Hackman—but everyone's in the movie *together;* it's not a vehicle for *anybody.*

"When I saw that it was going to be treated that way, all my fears about commercialism vanished. I mean, no one is forcing this interpretation down my throat. If I say, 'Please, one more take, I want to change something'—they do it."

What about the myriad of books, records, toys and T-shirts to come? Wouldn't he begin to feel like a product?

"We haven't got on to the merchandising end of it yet—how I'll feel having my face splashed on posters and this and that and the other. But I feel it's the *character* they're selling . . . it's not me. I think people will take you for who you say you are. I'll say, 'Hello, my name's Christopher Reeve and I'm delighted to play Superman,' and *boom!*—I give it my full effort. But at five o'clock, I hang up my cape and go home. People will come to understand that. I went to a kid's birthday party the other day, as a matter of fact, and they'd all been told that Superman was coming to the party. And I walked in wearing corduroys and a lumber jacket,

and all the little kids said, 'Superman? Where's Superman?' and I just thought fast and said, 'Well, it's Saturday today, and my cape's in the wash. But I really *am*
Superman!' and it was O.K. For kids, I'll do that."

•   •   •

As principal production people began to trickle back
to Pinewood toward the end of November, there were
two main problems facing the film.

First, the schedule. A decision had been made back
in September by all the top production personnel, along
with Warner Brothers Vice President Charles Greenlaw
(now on the scene full time in an advisory capacity),
that the delivery date for the "answer print"—the initial
print of a completed film—would be April 15, 1978. But
in the months since the decision had been made, that
date had come to seem an impossibility, particularly
in view of what still had to be filmed—at least 95 major
flying shots (and the flying was continuing to cause sig-
nificant problems), dozens of complex model sequences,
and principal photography that would probably now
involve location work in Finland or Norway (more
glacier shots) and Spain (a desert road sequence). And
shooting still had not been resumed.

The second problem was money. As the production
went way over schedule and the budget soared, the flow
of cash had slowed down appreciably. And that, in turn,
slowed down everything on the film. Photo processing
almost came to a standstill. The owners of some of the
key flying unit equipment locked it in a safe until the
outstanding bills were paid. One of the outside construction companies threatened to bulldoze the model
of the Golden Gate Bridge on the back lot unless money
was forthcoming. Even the Superman T-shirts which
had been ordered for the crew had been impounded by
an irate freight company!

Though main-unit photography remained at a standstill, work had continued on some of the effects units.

Chris was putting in six-day (and even seven-day) weeks with the flying unit with whatever equipment was not under lock and key. I can imagine what would have happened to the film at this point if some high-powered, uncooperative superstar had been cast in the title role.

Model Unit 1 was back at work on the Golden Gate Bridge, which had a huge makeshift "pond" beneath it doubling for San Francisco Bay. Nearby, the unit, short of stage space, had improvised and taken the wooden top half of the balloon from the escape sequence in "Superman II" and turned it into a temporary shooting stage where story boards could be photographed. Exploring some "never before attempted" processes and methods, Derek Meddings told me that for this sequence he and the special-effects team would cut together footage shot over a period of several months on five separate locations—the actual bridge in San Francisco; two separate models in two sizes; Bovingdon Airfield in England, where a set of a lane of the bridge was photographed; and, finally, back-projection plates of the area beyond the bridge in California.

Model Unit 2 was filming shots of the world revolving, which was accomplished by photographing a large wood-and-plaster globular construction, meticulously painted, behind which black gauze had been hung to simulate the blackness of space.

During my first week back on the lot after my visit home, I dropped by the publicity office to find out the latest gossip.

There was still no clear story as to why the main unit had stopped shooting, Gordon Arnell told me, and no one seemed to know why Dick Donner had delayed his return to London.

On the brighter side, Arnell showed me a copy of the Christmas catalogue from the fashionable Texas department store, Sakowitz. As its "premier" gift for this Yuletide season, Sakowitz was offering a genuine "premiere"; for a mere $250,000, some lucky purchaser could secure a private screening of "Superman" at least one day before the world premiere. The price also included five-year screening rights for personal showings.

*   *   *

Pinewood was bursting at the seams these days, with several important productions shooting in addition to "Superman." "International Velvet"—a sequel to the classic "National Velvet"—starring Tatum O'Neal, was filming in and around the Pinewood complex. Just returned from eight weeks of shooting in Egypt was the latest Agatha Christie thriller, "Death on the Nile," with a cast that included Bette Davis, David Niven, Peter Ustinov and Mia Farrow. "Warlords of Atlantis," starring Doug McClure, would soon be returning from location in Malta, and a remake of "The Thirty-Nine Steps" was in pre-production. Since "Superman" dominated the studio facilities, space was at a premium. According to studio managing director Cyril Howard, Pinewood had been too booked up to accept the new "Pink Panther" film, which had gone before the cameras elsewhere. All good news for the British film industry.

*   *   *

Skye Salkind arranged a Thanksgiving celebration for the American contingent working on "Superman"— which at the moment meant Chris Reeve and me.

Thursday, naturally, was a regular working day in England, so Skye thoughtfully postponed her dinner—a roast turkey with all the traditional trimmings—until Sunday afternoon. Along with Ilya and Skye and their daughter Anastasia, the celebrants included Monique and Pierre Spengler, producer-director Blake Edwards (whose wife, Julie Andrews, was unfortunately in Los Angeles), American actor Bob Webber and his wife Del, and Maria Monreal and her young son Rodrigo.

As we were leaving the Salkinds', I asked Rodrigo how he had liked his first "American" Thanksgiving dinner. "Oh, very much, thank you," he replied in thickly accented English, "especially the *donkey!*"

•   •   •

Dick Donner had still not returned, and the official word was that the director was in Los Angeles suffering from major dental problems. Rumors sweeping the studio had it that Dick was more seriously ill; that he had abandoned the picture; that he was lining up with Warner Brothers to take over the whole production; even that he was hiding out somewhere in London! Ugly stories were being churned out in the trade publications that the producers, Dick and the distributors were engaged in battles over percentages, payments and guarantees.

Part of the explanation of Donner's absence—and of the whole mystery of the break in the shooting—was that the director *had* been meeting with the Warner brass in an effort to make them understand why the film had gone so far beyond schedule, and to convince them that it had to be completed without compromise and without jeopardizing the whole project.

Early in December, Dick returned to Pinewood and immediately devoted himself to viewing and cutting the backlog of effects work that had been shot while he was in the States. (He also screened a three-reel breakdown of the first rough assemblage of the film.) His office was a mass of charts and graphs, carefully blocking off crucial unit shots yet to be completed.

Soon Dick zeroed in on the flying work and began to spend most of his time on "A" stage, where Chris was finishing up a sequence in which he confronts a trio of hoodlums on a cabin cruiser. The director was also concerned about Wally Veevers' progress with the problematical front and back projection screens. Because the screens had to be enormous (they wrapped around the entire stage) but also mobile, Veevers had ordered them constructed in large square sections which could be assembled, taken down, and then reassembled according to the requirements of the shots. But it was all too clear from the rushes that the seams between the sections were visible in certain scenes. (Eventually, this key problem was solved by working closely with the 3M Company and actually coming up with a completely *new* type of FP material.)

• • •

Film make-up goes a long way beyond powder, wrinkle-concealers and hairdo's. For "Superman," it required Stuart, Kay and Graham Freeborn to fashion dozens of face casts, entire head casts, chest molds, full body molds (for the flying), and even animals—such as the polar bear—with moveable eyes, tongues and jaws (as Stu had done with the magnificent apes in "2001").

I enthusiastically accepted an invitation from the Freeborns to have a life-mask made of my face. The whole process took well over an hour, and it was easy to see why the Freeborns are lauded as the best in the business. (Stu had created nearly every fantastic creature in the famous "Star Wars" cantina sequence by hand!)

The steps for the face mask included application of a jellylike layer of Latex, which was then covered with layers of wet plaster, scrim (burlap) and gauze bandage. Stuart and Graham worked as quickly as possible, with the least amount of discomfort possible for their subject. Still, despite their efficiency, having the mask done made me reconsider my somewhat harsh past generalizations about pampered stars!

• • •

Not long after Dick Donner's return, high-level decisions were again being considered, relating to the delivery of the film. The break in main-unit shooting had now put the production hopelessly behind schedule, and Pierre was advising poor Alex to take a Valium before looking at each amended budget. But with all the discord and disagreement, the only decision that emerged was to postpone a decision.

As the picture seemed to be reaching a terminal crisis, the stories continued to spew out of Hollywood, with Rona Barrett calling Ilya personally to discuss the rumors that he and Skye were splitting up. "Nonsense!" retorted an annoyed Salkind, and Skye felt obliged to reiterate the denial in a friendly telephone call of her own to Ms. Barrett. There was no question in any of our minds, though, that the problems and pressures currently weighing on the young executive producer would put a strain on any marriage.

Happily, the Christmas season was now in full swing, and people's spirits picked up noticeably despite the tension on the set.

At the studio, there was a special lunch a few days before Christmas, followed by a convivial "drink-up" in the bar that same evening. I got properly sloshed, and big, burly Frank Elliot and Miki Thomas, from the camera crew of "Death on the Nile," picked me up by the elbows and set me on the nine-foot stone mantle above the fireplace. Someone else in the crowd grabbed a seltzer bottle and gave me a thorough dousing.

Christopher Reeve left to go back to New York for the holidays. To his chagrin (Chris is painfully shy about his Superman persona in public), the boys on the flying unit called the Concorde departure lounge at Heathrow and had a British Airways employee page Superman and deliver the following message: "Remember to keep your arms out straight and your feet together *so you won't crab!*"

On Christmas Day, the Salkinds gave a party, and after it we adjourned to the master bedroom to watch a telecast of "The Wizard of Oz," which Alex had never seen. The senior Salkind watched the film intently, paying particular attention to the elaborate effects, which he perceptively noted must have been a source of inspiration for George Lucas's "Star Wars." Alex seemed especially interested in Margaret Hamilton on her broomstick, with her legion of monkeys, flying through the air. "Ilya," he demanded, "how did they do that? . . . and back then!" Watching with us, with more than casual interest, was Skye's long-time friend Lorna Luft, the daughter of Judy Garland and Sid Luft, and she and I both cried as we heard her mother say, for the umpteenth time in our lives, "Auntie Em, there's no place like home!"

After that, it was a steady round of parties with the crew, with much good cheer and a hell of a lot of wassailing!

Poor Maria Monreal spent much of *her* free time tracking down an overland—that's right, *overland*—route from Europe to the United States for Alex Salkind so that the eccentric entrepreneur could attend a special benefit première of "Superman" in Washington, D.C., with Mrs. Jimmy Carter in attendance. Salkind's claustrophobic "fear of flying" meant that Maria—after consulting maps, a globe and her travel agent—had to come up with train connections that would transport Alex from Paris to Moscow, Moscow to Siberia, Siberia across the Bering Straits, across Canada and on to Washington . . . or something like that!

I suggested slipping Alex a mickey and putting him on a Concorde, and Maria replied that in view of the current state of the shooting schedule, they'd probably

—181—

all go to Washington for the premiere—and then come back to London to finish the film!

•   •   •

Now it was 1978. Shooting resumed on the Tuesday after New Year's with a retake of part of Superman's trial by fire in the tunnel leading to Luthor's lair.

A notable event of that first week of the New Year was Ilya's screening, for Jay Emmett, one of the Warner Communications chiefs, of the stunning thirty-second "Superman" teaser that had been rushed over from Los Angeles. The teaser would soon be running in a thousand theaters back in the States, letting audiences know that "Superman" was coming—with any luck, sometime in the foreseeable future.

After doing the reshoot on the tunnel—it was fascinating to watch Superman making his way through a hail of bullets, a veritable inferno, and a blinding snowstorm (tiny balls of styrofoam and well-placed wind machines)—the main unit concentrated on finishing up incomplete scenes. With chiefly effects work ahead and most of the big stars gone, the long days began to have an awful way of blending into each other, and the dreary gray winter weather didn't help much. At dusk, I often thought the studio back lot looked like some vast, eerie junk yard.

Over the weekend, a near tragedy and a real one took place.

The flying unit, working overtime on Saturday afternoon to complete several scenes, was just wrapping up a rehearsal when the wires keeping stuntman Paul Weston airborne suddenly snapped, and he went crashing to the floor of "A" stage forty feet below, missing the mattresses meant to minimize the danger of such an accident. But Weston, a trained stunt artist in top condition, knew how to fall (I've always been skeptical

of that phrase, but seeing is believing) and escaped
serious injury.

That same day, however, a young Pinewood metal
worker, Terry Hill, was killed in a freakish accident; he
was crushed under the wing of a mock-up of Air Force
One which collapsed.

As several people noted on Monday, when a collec-
tion was taken up for Hill's family, the new year was off
to a very inauspicious start.

Spirits lifted later in the week as word reached Pinewood that the teaser was already running in theaters in
America and receiving highly enthusiastic response.

Then the bomb dropped. Word reached the studio
that *Daily Variety* had carried a front-page story report-
ing that Warner Brothers, fearing late delivery of the
film due to the complicated special-effects work, had
pulled "Superman" from its summer release schedule
and rebooked it for Christmas, 1978!

The impact was electrifying. The Salkinds reacted
angrily at first, and issued a counterstatement, claiming
that delivery *could* in fact be made on schedule. However, behind the scenes, everything connected with the
release—premieres, public appearances, merchandising
tie-ins—was already being rescheduled. And everyone
on the picture privately admitted that the December
'78 release date was the only realistic alternative to com-
promising the film and risking disaster.

The aftershock of the story spawned hundreds of
fresh rumors and once again Rona Barrett didn't miss
the opportunity to tell her coast-to-coast audience that
since "everyone could see the wires holding up Superman," Warner Brothers had had no choice but to rebook
the film and try to iron out the problem. That wasn't
the part of her story that bothered the producers or
Dick Donner, however.

What did get their hackles up was Barrett's state-
ment that Warner Brothers had taken over control of

—183—

the film and that, in effect, the Salkinds and Spengler were merely hired employees of the distributor.

On top of everything else, problems with the actual physical production of the film continued to multiply. A vast cloud of uncertainty descended over the entire project.

• • •

The main unit was now making preparations to re-shoot the exterior cat-in-the-tree scene. Since I knew that whatever useable footage they already had had been shot outdoors in Brooklyn Heights in 90-degree weather—and here we were in England in the dead of winter—I wondered how the matching problem would be solved.

Filming on the retake of the sequence began, with the front of the Pinewood administration block doctored up with plastic brick, vinyl flagstone and trees with fake wired-on leaves, an effort to make it resemble a row of New York brownstones. Ten or twelve American cars, hired locally, were parked outside, but it wasn't until one of the final rehearsals that someone noticed that the cars still had European license plates, and dummy U.S. plates were quickly substituted.

The first night's shooting began in a light but steady mixture of sleet and rain—and this scene had to match with a "fly-in" shot filmed in New York in those July temperatures. No wonder the call sheet asked for "protective clothing and thermal underwear for artistes"!

Another switch from Brooklyn Heights was the use of three white Devon Rex cats, in addition to a stuffed one. And despite all the adversities that first night, one of the live cats gave a Patsy Award-winning performance, staying immobilized in one of the prop trees for the whole evening.

For the next two nights of shooting, crew members huddled around fires to keep warm. On the third night a dense pea-soup fog brought "Superman," and most of greater London, to a grinding halt. At last, after almost an entire week of working under hardship conditions, Dick was satisfied that it was a wrap on "cat in the tree." (As I write this, a debate is going on in the cutting rooms as to whether the entire scene should be excised from the picture! Such are the changing fates of films.)

The other units, meanwhile, were engrossed in special-effects shooting, with several of the crews shifting to shots usually outside the scope of their normal duties—the flying unit, for instance, was working on an explosion in space. While one of the model units was experimenting with infrared light and lasers for the effects needed for the journey of Kal-El's starship through space, the other was busy filming scenes of the XK 101 missiles. I was fascinated as Derek Meddings explained some of the "magic" to me.

Against a giant sky-blue canvas backdrop, several different-sized models—roughly two, three and four feet long—were anchored. They were then backlit (to increase contrast) and emitted CO_2 gas to simulate their exhaust trails. Mirrors positioned nearby were used to achieve apparent changes in the rockets' trajectories.

The camera was suspended on wires for maximum maneuverability; in front of it Derek had placed a device involving two large revolving Plexiglas disks, operated by chain belt and motor, onto which cloud patterns had been spray-painted. Photographing the rockets through the spinning disks, camera operator John Morgan was able to come up with a convincing image of the missiles hurtling through the clouds. To simulate the rockets' distant contrails far off in space, Derek had devised an ingenious technique employing what looked like a small syringe. The syringe, moved by Derek's black-gloved hand across a horizontal glass plate with black velvet underneath it, released a trail of salt upon the glass.

The flying unit took up where the model unit had left off on the Golden Gate Bridge sequence and began filming scenes of Superman flying to the rescue. Before they could start, however, a section of the enormous bridge model had to be moved, and the giant crane used in the balloon sequence was again brought in. But someone had neglected to tell the crane operator that the section of the bridge to be moved was secured *in concrete,* so that when he attempted to shift it, the crane's massive metal cables snapped, delaying the shooting until they could be repaired.

Once more the main unit was on night shooting, filming yet another retake in the tunnel leading to Luthor's lair, a portion of which had been constructed on the lot behind the production office. The scene, Superman's progress through a raging fire, was to be intercut with front-projected footage of an asbestos-treated manne-quin of Chris. However, Reeve had physically devel-oped so much since the mannequin had been made that his muscular physique cast a shadow on the projection clip over the spot where the "dummy" had been. A new mannequin had to be made and the whole process repeated from scratch.

Before Donner and the main unit shifted yet again, I stopped by "C" stage one morning to see Martin Grace —he had done some flying stunt work on "Superman"— who, Pinewood's p.r. man Norman Martlew had told me, would be spending the next two days oiled up in a scant bikini swimsuit, posing for the first reshoot of the world-famous Rank Organisation symbol, the Man with the Gong!

•   •   •

The production was now well into February, and all the units were making slow but steady progress, even in the face of a Pinewood slowdown that banned over-time work.

Perhaps things were getting back to normal just a bit too much, because no one seemed to notice when a would-be robber, armed with a plastic pistol, made his way into the accounts department at lunchtime one Friday—perhaps he read the trades and wanted to share in the production's apparent largesse?—holding one of the employees, George Cox, at "gunpoint" while he rummaged in the office for loot. After a few frustrating minutes, he escaped with nothing, ignoring the stack of tiny envelopes that contained the weekly payroll. After this, people took to locking their office doors.

The flying unit was now working with some natural-born experts, a golden eagle, two Lanner falcons, and a Saker falcon, which were being used to film a majestic sequence of Superman soaring through the sky with an eagle. (Shades of John Denver!) The Saker falcon was the one finally used and the scene went well; conditioned to fly toward the lights and then return to its trainer's arm, the bird performed beautifully.

On "F" stage, Model Unit 1 was still working on the missile sequences. The construction crew had built a camera track along the entire length of the stage; and, except for the area immediately around the camera, the whole stage had been hung in black velvet cloth to block out any peripheral light. By tracking the camera backward and forward, the illusion of movement was created more effectively than by simply using a zoom lens alone. The track had been carefully marked with tape at precisely measured intervals, and a.d. Gareth Tandy, using a flashlight, would call out the distances as guides to the camera crew. But every now and then, working in the pitch dark, the men pulling the camera platform would misjudge and ram into the stage wall.

Later the model unit moved outdoors into bitterly cold, windy weather to shoot exterior rocket shots. During one take I witnessed, the missile, powered by a flarelike charge and traveling along a wire, shot past the

camera and disappeared across the road toward the 007
stage—almost impaling a startled passerby on a motor
scooter, who circled back to find out what the hell had
whizzed by him!

• • •

The third week in February, Dick Donner and the
producers scheduled a celebration on the North Tunnel
stage to mark the first anniversary of Christopher Reeve's
signing his contract to play Superman. Again there was
a big cake and plenty of booze. The crew seemed to be
in good spirits—particularly the ever-ebullient Donner—
enjoying the time-out from the breakneck schedule, talking about everything from the Begelman scandals in
Hollywood to the John Williams "movie music" concert
at the Royal Albert Hall the previous evening to the fact
that many of them had been working together for a year
or more now.

Despite the grueling year he'd been through, Chris
Reeve looked unusually fit. He had gained weight, all
of it muscle, and his physique was marvelously well
developed. (Standing next to Reeve, I noticed that his
thigh alone was about as big as my entire body. It's
awful to be just a thigh!)

Not long after the Reeve commemorative fete, another
shindig marked the near-completion of *my* first year on
the shooting. This one was given by my English publicist, the celebrated London hostess Lila Burkeman, at
her posh apartment. Among the luminaries in attendance were, along with the "Superman" heavyweights
(Margot once again in "haute punk"), producer-director
Norman Jewison, "Death on the Nile" star Simon
MacCorkindale, *Screen International's* chatty Editor-in-
Chief, Peter Noble, and a host of other European celebrities. I reveled in every star-studded minute of it and
dreamed that night that the next day's headline in
Daily Variety read: "YANKEE SCRIBE FETED IN

BLIGHTY! TINSEL TOWN AWAITS TRIUMPHANT
RETURN!"

•   •   •

Toward the end of February, the weather turned even
colder and David Tomblin, working outside in near-
freezing temperatures on the still incomplete helicopter
crash, remarked that he was convinced no film could go
on this long. We were all dead, he assured me, and this
was Hell!

Passing the make-up rooms one day, I noticed that
some joker had stuck a supersize phallus on one of
Graham Freeborn's Superman models. I think everybody was beginning to flip out a bit.

Over on "E" stage, an enormous blue screen, larger
than any used earlier on the film for matte shots, had
been erected for some panoramic flying sequences. Because of all the lighting needed to shoot on the stage,
two massive fans, nearly two stories tall with protective
metal mesh around them, were employed at both the
main entrances. This was necessary, Roy Field told me,
to draw out smoke from the heat of the brutes that
would otherwise create a veil against the blue backing
which the cameras would pick up.

On "C" stage, I watched the main unit prepare to
shoot the scene in which Lois Lane's car is caught in a
narrowing fissure during the earthquake.

In one of the most elaborate mechanical setups of the
entire film, the car had been wedged into a huge V-
shaped compressing device, like a gigantic trash masher,
that was operated by hydraulic mechanisms on either
side.

The V was lined with large chunks of earth, rocks,
and pieces of foam rubber sprayed black and brown
and sprinkled with thousands of clay pellets.

Cameras had been mounted at every imaginable
angle around the car, which meant that getting to them

was something of a gymnastic feat. The scene on the stage prior to each rehearsal and take amounted to controlled chaos, as Dick and camera operator Gordon Hayman crawled about the specially constructed rostrum to check each camera setup.

I watched several takes of Margot being very nearly literally compressed in the car.

"What was most uncomfortable, actually," a slightly battered, clay-encrusted Kidder told me later, collapsing in her chair, "was having all that dirt down my throat! When I coughed, I was spitting it right out! Dirt in my ears, in my eyes, in my nose. . . ."

Margot spat out a few remaining pellets.

"It was like reliving an awful childhood experience. When I was a kid in Labrador, I was trapped in a car for *eight hours!* But the shooting was kind of like Gestalt therapy. I exorcised the old fears—'acted' them out, literally! Maybe I'm an actress because I'm trying to get rid of these fears, to get rid of my past. Who knows?"

Margot spat out more dirt.

"When they started filming the scene with me in the car, I had my head against the protective roll bar. Dick yelled, 'Action!' and the hydraulic presses began crushing the car. Actually, it was crushed in three stages. The windows went first, of course. Then they stopped the presses and began pouring *more* dirt on me by the *bagsful*—little clay pellets. I was more concerned about the shattering glass, though. Dick assured me that it was covered by plastic sheeting, which would prevent the shards from flying. I wasn't so sure!

"So then I had to start screaming, you know, pleading for help. And then I tried to climb out of the car. And I thought a good touch would be to grab onto the rear view mirror in my attempt to get out. So I *did* grab on—and it came off in my hands! Naturally, I fell back in the seat on my butt. Well, Donner loved it and decided to keep it as part of the action."

Leaving Margot still spitting out little chunks of dirt, I wandered back to the stage where Model Unit 2 was shooting an atomic explosion.

Sometimes the "magic" of movie-making is just a bit disquieting when you discover that what looks and sounds phenomenal on the screen was accomplished by some simple—albeit clever—means.

To create the explosion effect, Les Bowie and his team designed an eight-foot-tall glass tank, which was filled with water. At the top of the tank, a billowy cloudlike pattern had 'been spray-painted on the glass. A board covered the open top of the tank and through a center hole in it, a bulb attached to a dimmer control (and to a rod that served as a line-up guide) had been inserted. On cue, one of the crew members poured diluted white paint through the hole as the dimmer switch turned the bulb to full brightness. Being heavier than water, the paint sank and mushroomed out at the bottom of the tank. Filming this with an inverted camera created the impression of a rising column of "smoke" with the familiar atomic mushroom at the top.

• • •

It was now almost March and the first new growth of spring—my *second* spring on "Superman"—dotted the broad fields around Pinewood.

I was told that despite the possibility of more principal photography on location, and though there was still much special-effects work to be done, we might wrap as early as May—if the pace suddenly changed for the better.

I was dubious. I had noted, taped to the side of one of the cameras, along with the chronology of the other films photographed by this particular camera, an addendum: "Superman—1977 & 1978 & 1979 & 1980 & 1981 . . ." Was it possible that someone knew something about this picture that *I* didn't?

11
Millions and millions more
—and still counting

Of course, the pace didn't change for the better—there was no reason to think that it would. But I comforted Dick, Ilya and Pierre with the reassuring information that they still had a long way to go before they beat the record for the longest production schedule. That questionable honor belonged by a technicality to Abel Gance's epic "Bonaparte," the first version of which started shooting in 1927, using a three-screen process that theaters were not equipped for until a final, edited cut of the film appeared in March, 1977—*fifty years* later! (Ironic, that that film should finish as "Superman" started.)

However, since many a truth is said in jest, we all had mixed reactions to the "Important Notice" taped to the production office door: "The management regrets it has come to their attention that employees dying on this production are failing to fall over. This practice must stop, as it becomes impossible to distinguish between death and natural movement of the unit. Any member found dead in an upright position will be dropped from the payroll immediately." The notice was signed, ostensibly by Dick Donner.

● ● ●

With so many crucial scenes yet to be shot, Donner decided to call a halt to the "trial and error" tactics characterizing much of the experimental effects work and simply concentrate on what shots were absolutely necessary to the integrity of the film.

Decisions came fast. For one thing, the idea of additional shooting on glacial fields in Finland or Norway was scrubbed—the existing footage would have to suffice. But it was also decided, after numerous tests on the back lot, that the only way to shoot the desert road sequence—the last major scene of principal photography —was on location. Spain was considered, as were other possibilities in Europe, but Donner opted for the real thing and shooting was set for the New Mexico desert outside Gallup, some time in May.

All the schedule reshuffling and the new delivery date of "Superman" called for delicate tightrope-walking by many key people on the film who were committed to other projects now imminent. For a tense week or two, it looked as if composer John Williams would have to bow out. John had screened a rough assemblage of the picture in early March, but many essential scenes were still incomplete—and John likes to work from a finished print. Returning to London at a later date seemed out of the question, as he had been booked to score several other films that would pose a conflict. But after talks with the Warner people, Donner and the producers, Williams agreed to juggle his schedule, start working on the film from the story boards, and come back in July to record with the London Symphony Orchestra, as he had done with "Star Wars."

Despite all the work still ahead, the production team had to consider the many highly specialized areas of post-production, a phase in the process of filmmaking perhaps less exciting but every bit as important as principal photography. Without question, the most important task after the cameras have stopped turning is the editing.

Because of the sheer volume of "Superman" footage, the editing had been an ongoing process for Stuart Baird and his crack crew. The pace became even more frantic—if that was possible—in the last few months before a final answer print was ready.

Working with an enormous team of some *eighteen* editorial staffers, the affable Baird—his perpetual pallor now accented by his red-rimmed eyes—could almost always be found holed away in his darkened office at the back of the cutting rooms, poring over footage running through the moviola while classical music blared from his cassette recorder.

"My job is to get the best out of the material the director has shot," Baird told me during a quick lunchtime chat. "If the scene is too long, we cut it down. The director maybe has seven takes of a scene, and he may say which he thinks is the best. Then it's left to the editor to make the most of the scene . . . to get across the best dramatic point, or the comedy, or the poignancy or whatever.

"Every director is different. Sometimes the editor makes recommendations that a certain scene should go, because it's slowing the pace. And often the director won't want to see that because he's in love with *every* shot. Dick isn't like that at all. He knows what he wants, sure, but he's open to advice . . . even criticism. And Dick realizes that the editor, because he hasn't shot the material, can often be more objective.

"As far as the actual filmmaking process goes, the cutting room is the center of everything—all the footage has to be sorted out there. It's up to the editors to make it work in both the visual and the audio sense—sound effects, dialogue, music, all crucial to the total effect of the film.

"On this film, there are so many more departments than there would be on an ordinary film—first unit, second units, flying, model, plate and matte units . . . a mountain of optical work. All of this has to be coordinated by the cutting rooms."

Baird sighed. " 'Superman' has presented us with many special problems, the greatest being the sheer amount of material. The bulk of the actual slogging work is being done as the picture is shot. Otherwise it would pile up so much that at the end it would be impossible to deal with. Another special problem has been waiting for the optical sequences to be completed. You can't judge a scene totally until *all* the material is in."

Baird sighed again. "It's been a twelve-hour-a-day, often seven-days-a-week job," he said, and looking at the exhaustion in his face, I had no reason to doubt his words. "This is perhaps the most complex movie ever made. Some of the most innovative special effects ever achieved on film have been accomplished for 'Superman.' The number of effects shots is staggering. That's why I have to be careful about pacing the film. I believe that in the editing stages, you have to get on with the story. That doesn't mean you go at a galloping pace all the way through it; there are times when one wants to hold a shot, because the audience, although they might not consciously realize it, wants that shot held. You have to know how to hold back, and then—wham! —you have to know where to hit them with something powerful. These are things you learn through experience . . . they really can't be taught."

Now the important question: Would *my* big scene stay in the film?

Stuart gulped down his last bit of lunch, rose from the table, and hesitated a moment. "I . . . uh . . . really don't know yet. We'll have to see what happens over the next few months. But if it's in, you'll even have a close-up."

He smiled diplomatically before he drifted off in a rather suspicious hurry toward the cutting rooms.

On my way to "F" stage to watch tests of the burning starship traveling through space, I bumped into Ilya

Salkind, bubbling with the good news that Skye had just given birth to a baby boy—Sebastian James—in Los Angeles. I congratulated him and, mindful of what Stuart Baird had said, went off to Roy Field's office to discuss the optical work.

All through the shooting, I had heard the same line on the floor, in the cutting rooms and in Dick Donner's office: "This is going to be done optically." What precisely did that mean? I asked Roy.

"Opticals," Roy explained in his usual soft-spoken way, "are a means of manipulating film once it's exposed, by printing various elements together and introducing other components, such as overlays, to achieve a certain visual effect. We break it down into sections. We deal with principal photography first, then with the edited pieces of film. Take the Air Force One sequence, for example. The plane is traveling through the storm and lightning strikes it. Well, first they shoot the plane going through the clouds. Then they say, 'O.K., now let's give it to Roy Field.' And I take what's been shot and give it to the optical artist. He paints the lightning on glass, and then that is photographed with the film frame behind it to make the composite image. You start with a thin streak, then a thicker one, and you do that with seven or eight frames—as many as you need to get the effect you want."

Field nodded toward the schedules piled on his desk. "One of the biggest problems with optical work is time. And we're so pushed already. 'Star Wars' had something like three hundred eighty optical shots, I read. We'll wind up with well over a hundred more than that—maybe two hundred more. But quantity isn't what matters here. It's quality—and that takes time . . . and money.

"A major flying sequence in 'Superman' involves live action, front or perhaps back projection, traveling matte and quite probably opticals. All this gives the effects teams greater freedom to achieve exactly what Dick

Donner wants. Certainly there are limitations. But I believe that by combining the best of all these processes, *anything* is possible."

•　　　•　　　•

The next day I saw rushes of the tests on the flaming starship, and thought it looked like a low-budget Fourth of July fireworks display. Dick obviously wasn't pleased either. Looking at the blazing model in the darkened theater, he started singing, "Happy birthday to you, happy birthday to you. . . ." That, of course, meant more tests, and a reshoot.

Whether there would be time to reshoot that, or anything else, seemed debatable, as rumors were rampant in the production office to the effect that Alexander Salkind had watched the budget come perilously close to the cost of World War II, had held an emergency three-way telephone conference with Ilya and Pierre, and was now at the end of his financial rope. As a result, according to the rumors, *all* shooting—with the exception of the flying—would be halted and a final cut would be made from the existing footage.

Again, the prophets of doom on the film went into general panic, but by now crisis had become the norm on "Superman" and each successive upheaval was, by and large, greeted with a greater degree of equanimity.

The Warner Brothers chiefs back in Burbank, however, didn't take that kind of talk so calmly—not with their multi-million-dollar distribution deal on the line. And since they were so impressed by the footage they'd seen and didn't want to jeopardize the project, several hasty phone calls were made to Alexander Salkind, who was more concerned than anyone else about preserving the integrity of his film. Happily, an arrangement was made by which Warner Brothers would come up with additional money, basically as an advance against Salkind's royalties. That way, "Superman" could be completed exactly as Richard Donner envisaged.

The rest of March, and most of April and May, saw the completion of unfinished scenes, dozens of required reshoots, and more special-effects work.

A huge reconstruction of a portion of Boulder Dam had been built on the back lot, complete with hairline fissures ready to burst, and rigged from behind with a jungle of hosing connected to the studio water lines so that a high-pressure near-tidal wave could gush on cue. An expertly crafted model—about fifteen feet high, complete with mini-generators, cables, roads, cars, houses and all the features of the terrain surrounding the dam —had been built so that even more realistic shots of the dam bursting after the earthquake could be accomplished. The main problem, of course, was waiting for blue sky, to match what had already been shot on location in the States.

There had also been some additional work on the Fortress of Solitude set, which still had not been entirely struck from the 007 stage (though the enormous plywood figure of Superman, which had hung on the stage the previous autumn, had come down).

●   ●   ●

Director Steven Spielberg and John Williams, fresh from the triumphant Royal Premiere of "Close Encounters of the Third Kind" in London, paid a brief visit to the Fortress set and then went off with Margot and Christopher for lunch.

Shortly after the opening of Spielberg's blockbuster, another film that had been burning up the box office back in the States—"Saturday Night Fever"—premiered in London. The Robert Stigwood Organization staged a glittering opening night, including a screening of the film, with John Travolta in well-guarded attendance,

—198—

and a lavish buffet supper and party afterwards at a local disco, where such revellers as Bianca Jagger, the Who's Keith Moon, David Frost, Peter Sellers, Rachel Roberts, and Joan Collins boogied till dawn. Ignoring the merrymaking, Ilya and Pierre spent a good part of the evening huddled in a corner analyzing the fact that this relatively low-budget film had obviously touched a highly sensitive public nerve and was keeping pace with the current mega-million movie champs—certainly something for them to ponder.

• • •

Because of shaky plate work in New York City and the need for additional scenes, a section of the side of the Solow Building in Manhattan had been constructed parallel to the floor on "E" stage. Here Superman would be shown collaring a would-be robber as he attempts to scale the glass-faced building. To add to the expense, Donner had to send for New York actor David Baxt, who had played the burglar some ten months before in Manhattan.

After more than a week's work on this set, yet another farewell drink-up was organized, this time for the highly respected Geoffrey Unsworth and his camera crew. Not imagining that "Superman" would still be shooting well into 1978, Geoff had long ago committed himself to a new production, Michael Crichton's "The Great Train Robbery," that was now about to begin principal photography in Ireland. A sentimental Dick Donner and Unsworth embraced, the latter assuring the director that he'd be back in July to do post-production work on "Superman."

In early April, Ilya Salkind arranged a get-together at his Mayfair home to watch the 50th Academy Awards show, taped a day earlier in California. Watching producers Charles Joffee and Jack Rollins accept the Best

Picture award for Woody Allen's "Annie Hall," Ilya was silent for a moment—and then he smiled. "Next year," he said with conviction, "that'll be us!"

A few days after the Awards show, Dick was able to get a print of the film many people had been hoping would walk away with an armload of Oscars—"Close Encounters of the Third Kind." Nearly everyone connected with "Superman" showed up for the screening. The special-effects experts, along with Stuart Baird and Christopher Reeve, all seemed to be engrossed in the film, particularly its last effect-filled twenty minutes. "Very impressive," Stuart whispered to me in the darkness, admiring the superb model work.

The high-quality special effects of the Spielberg film reinforced the secrecy mania that seemed to be sweeping the "Superman" production, probably the result of recent stories in the trade press, both in England and abroad, claiming that the film was at a standstill because of effects difficulties. The director and the producers made a move to counter the canards.

Dick issued a memo: "I love you all and everything is going super. The gimmicks are totally ours, so please notify me if anybody from any publication, newspaper or magazine wants to do any pictures or interviews. I'll be only too happy to help you do them, but please clear it with me before anything is given out. The magic is still ours—let's keep it that way. Thanks." The memo was signed, playfully: "John Frankenheimer."

Then it was Ilya's turn, and his directive pointed out that the press "is trying to use whatever it can coming out from our production: gossip, rumor or hearsay, anything which can minimize our efforts," and went on to state that it would be "an enormous plus for the impact of the first openings if we keep our secrets to ourselves."

The new ban on visitors extended to people involved in other productions at Pinewood as well, and since the studio was crowded again after a brief lull—even Tatum O'Neal was back for additional shooting on "International Velvet"—Bob Simmonds again cautioned the a.d.'s to politely escort all intruders off the sets.

Toward the end of April, the weather seemed improved enough for Model Unit 1 to attempt blowing the model dam. The unit spent the better part of the day making sure the set was properly dressed, that all six cameras were in position and operating properly (John Morgan and Jonathan Taylor were stationed in what looked like a duck blind to protect them and their equipment from debris and rushing water), and that everything was ready for the big blowup. Of course, by the time all the preparations *were* complete, it had started to rain, so the shooting was scrubbed. In fact, the spectacular sequence was delayed for another fifteen days because of inclement weather; and when the dam finally did blow, it had to be photographed in two separate phases, since the plaster model of the dam had been so well constructed that even the carefully designed blasting devices failed to bring it crumbling down in one explosion—a circumstance which, happily, resulted in a far more believable shot.

In the bitter weather, most of us envied the special film crew working on "Superman" in sunny Bermuda under the supervision of Oxford Scientific Films, assigned to film oceanic plankton underwater to be used as "galactic images" in the space travel scenes.

These weather delays pushed the recently revised schedule back even further, and though obviously beyond anyone's control, didn't do much to warm up the cold war still existing between Dick Donner and the producers' office.

Since the rainy weather had delayed shooting on the dam mock-up on the back lot, Chris Reeve moved into the weather-cover set on "C" stage to shoot the complicated sequence of Superman traveling through the molten interior of the Earth to secure the shifting tectonic plates of California after the quake. The set involved a series of tunnels and passageways lined with dummy boulders, foil and other reflective materials, all painstakingly lit by cinematographer Alex Thompson so that a realistic impression of flowing lava and volcanic intensity would be achieved.

I hoped our own cinematic volcano would soon be erupting on movie screens around the world.

12

Look! Up on the screen! It's a bird! It's a plane! It's about time!

All through May, the special-effects shooting on "Superman" continued at Pinewood Studios, but now, for the first time, a completion date was in sight. Work didn't slow down on the film; the number of units simply decreased and there was less of a rainbow of multicolored call sheets on my desk every day.

The latest advance schedule called for the main unit to finish in New Mexico in June, the model units to complete shooting in late July, and the flying and traveling matte units to wrap the picture sometime in early August. The post-synching would continue at the Goldwyn Studios in Los Angeles throughout most of June, in early July, John Williams would return to England to record the entire film score with the London Symphony Orchestra. Stuart Baird and his team hoped to have an answer print by late September or early October; then would come a few carefully monitored previews in America—and finally the Washington premiere.

Dick Donner had gone to Los Angeles at the end of April to begin the post-synchronization work with Marlon Brando. Even as he returned to Pinewood, the top brass of Warner Brothers—chairman Ted Ashley, vice-chairman John Calley, and Bob Shapiro, vice president in charge of production—arrived in England for the kick-off of Stanley Kubrick's latest, "The Shining." First, however, they saw an almost four-hour screening of the latest assemblage of the "Superman" footage.

The reaction of the Warner execs was unanimous and overwhelmingly enthusiastic.

Three days after the screening, Donner received the following cable from the Burbank Studios, which he promptly circulated to the entire production:

"Dear Dick: I feel compelled to repeat what I said both in person and by telephone concerning 'Superman.' The picture is absolutely brilliant and so is the cast. I know how very hard all of them, yourself, and the crew, have worked. All of that work will wind up on the screen not only to the delight of the audiences but to the deep satisfaction of everybody who had a hand in making this great movie. As I reported to you and Margot, I tried to reach Chris Reeve several times, but his phone didn't answer. I would therefore particularly appreciate your conveying my compliments to him. As the general of the army, you deserve the biggest salute of all. With deepest appreciation and warmest personal regards. Ted Ashley."

The Warner chiefs had also given Dick the good news that since they thought the film didn't have "a dull moment," the director had their blessings to let it run as long as he felt was necessary. To the much harried Donner, this was a godsend.

As the main unit, now cut back to only a handful of key British technicians, prepared for the location work in New Mexico, the producers carried the news of the Warner reaction to the film to yet another Cannes Festival. A glowing Alexander Salkind conveyed the word to his anxious financial backers and to the distributors outside the Warner aegis, who had staked small fortunes on exhibiting "Superman." Once again, the Salkinds fleet of hired planes took to the skies above La Croisette, this time trailing banners which read: "SUPERMAN—PRINCIPAL PHOTOGRAPHY COMPLETED" (Well, almost completed.)

Just prior to Dick Donner's departure for Gallup, New Mexico, with Chris, Margot, Marc McClure and the English skeleton crew, word came from the location production manager, Tim Hampton, that in a freak storm six inches of snow had fallen on Gallup. One last time, Mother Nature had flexed her muscle to the detriment of "Superman."

The weather finally improved in Gallup, and the main unit departed.

For the units remaining at the studio, there was a full shooting schedule to cover the two to three weeks that Donner would be on location. Included were additional flying and matte work with the stunt team, more shots of the starship, explosions, on the Air Force One wing, as well as a new sequence involving Superman outracing the fastest commercial airliner in the world, the Concorde (in which Ilya and Pierre were set to play the French pilots!).

•   •   •

Reassuring word came from New Mexico. Amazingly, everything was going smoothly; shooting was almost right on the mark. So after what seemed like only a few days, Donner, Chris and the crew were back in Iver Heath. Dick enthusiastically screened the footage of the location work, all of which—especially the wide-angle crane shots of the New Mexico desert—seemed to justify the additional million dollars it had cost.

•   •   •

As "Superman" shooting continued into the summer and my publisher's deadline rapidly approached (they would need my manuscript before the film actually wrapped), I tried to sort out the million-and-one things

I still felt obliged to do, before heading back to Los Angeles.

I was tickled to get a call from the dubbing department in the cutting rooms to do post-synch work on my single line. I thought it might be a parting put-on, but sound editors Len Green and Stan Fiferman assured me that it was on the level, and even went so far as to run the footage of my scene through the moviola so that I could be properly motivated.

Certainly I felt that I should talk again with Christopher Reeve. I met him on "A" Stage, where he was still stoically practicing his demanding aerial gymnastics, and then we walked to the restaurant. In the administration building, we passed a corridor lined with color stills from "Superman"—a sure sign the film was almost completed.

"I don't know if people really care about Christopher Reeve the man, what motivates me, what my aspirations are," reflected the young actor, who was probably soon to be the biggest thing since sliced bread. "What people really want to see is the character. They want to look at the screen and say, 'Yeah, that's Superman!'

"When I started this whole game of being Superman, people said to me, 'How did a kid from New Jersey make the transition to Superman?' 'Well,' I said, 'you go to the audition, get the job and go to work.' 'Oh yeah,' they said, 'we see.' People come in, and I say, 'Well, I put on the costume and I stood on the kitchen table and then I flew around the room. . . . you know? And they say, 'Oh yeah, I bet you feel pretty *powerful!*' They're just playing out *their* fantasies, you know. And it must come out so boring that here's this guy who's just a kid from drama school and wangled himself a part in a big movie. They just don't know what to do with it. I'm going to have a really good time watching them all squirm because I'm *not* doing anything outrageous with my life."

Yet aren't *all* public figures accountable to their public?

"Everybody's got the right to be who they are," Reeve

replied. "The public has the right to look for 'spicy' stories, if that's what it wants. And I have the right to say what I want to say, always. I'm not avoiding anything—it's just that I'm not going to doctor myself up to fit some-body's else's picture of me. At the moment, I'm saved from the confusion of who *I* am and who the Superman character is, and I hope I can keep it that way."

How had Reeve's education, his preparation for a career, helped to bring about his present composed state of mind?

"I'm not sure. I think it has more to do with the dis-tance you have to travel emotionally from being obscure to bring prominent. And I think—this is not an easy thing to say—that I've always known I'd be in the lime-light. I knew I'd be a success. I simply never had any doubt about it. People were saying to me when I was fifteen, 'If you play your cards right, you'll be able to do what you want to do. So think about it, because you'll be able to make choices.' With so many people, life seems to 'happen' to them. Whereas with me . . . I 'happen' to life. So far, that's been the case. So if that's true, then I have the responsibility to use that power intelligently. Be-cause there are millions of people who'd give their eye-teeth for the same things, and the breaks aren't happen-ing that way for them.

"As I said, I knew from an early age that I was going to get someplace; I sensed it, and I worked for it. And that's fortunate. Take Freddie Prinz, for example. The distance he had to travel emotionally, from the tough West Side of New York to stardom in Hollywood at the age of twenty or twenty-one—it was too much for him, the distance was too great. Like the cliche says, it was too much, too soon, and it freaked him out. Whereas I've 'groomed' myself by saying, 'The way is this and this, and that and that, and study this and study that,' knowing all the time in my heart of hearts that I was going to make it. Then, when you *do* make it, you say, 'Great.

Thanks a lot.' And then come the detractors who say, 'He came out of nowwhere.' I *didn't* come out of nowhere. Because in my own admittedly egotistical brain I'd been saying, 'Just name the day, because it *is* going to happen.' When I got Superman, my agent couldn't believe it. As far as he was concerned, it was the biggest thing that could've happened. And my reaction, right off the bat, was, 'Yeah, fine. Now, when do I go to London? When do I start work?'"

Leaving the restaurant, we noticed how packed it was with wheeling and dealing producers, directors and costumed extras. "Superman" was nearing the end of shooting, and other films were crowding into Pine-wood to take its place.

* * *

Post-production on "Superman"—the editing, the dub-bing, the scoring—would begin in earnest now, but I would not be able to report its progress; my manuscript deadline had arrived.

I had begun work with "Superman" back in October, 1975. I had now spent sixteen months in England; I had logged more than 30,000 miles following the filming.

It had taken more than 350 actual shooting days to make "Superman." More than a thousand people had spent —who *knows* how many millions of dollars? (But, after all, most of "Superman II" had also been made!) A staggering 1,250,000 feet of film had been shot, of which only about 12,000 feet would become the finished print.

I thought it prophetic that I finished up in England on the Fourth of July. The day was marked on the set when Chris's driver brought him a hamburger wrapped in red, white and blue paper, and he and Donner were ser-enaded on the stage by crew members singing a medley of rousing Yankee tunes. I hurried back to Lon-don to host a traditional back-yard barbecue—in the rain, of course!—complete with hot dogs, hamburgers, and fireworks supplied by Colin Chilvers and Ron Burton from Special Effects.

•　　•　　•

As I write now, much of the best of the "Superman" story is yet to be told. Plans call for an old-fashioned, star-studded world premiere in December, in Washington, D.C.—black ties, limousines, klieg lights, maybe even a few laser beams piercing the night sky. The occasion will benefit the Kennedy Foundation's Special Olympics (a project to assist retarded children), and Mrs. Jimmy Carter will be the honorary chairperson. Within the week there will be openings in New York, Boston, Chicago and Los Angeles—and, of course, a Royal Premiere in London. By then, I'm sure, all the trials and tensions of an arduous production will have been forgotten, and all those concerned with the making of "Superman" will be enjoying the applause that greets a huge success.

For the moment, everything seems to be pointing to that great success. Whether it will be achieved is open to speculation. "It had *better* be," says Ilya Salkind, becoming visibly tense, "or my new address will be somewhere in South America!"

Of course, the ultimate judgement belongs, as it should to the world's critics: the audience. And, like them, I'll reserve my own opinion until the lights dim and the curtain goes up in Washington this December.

So, far from being the end of the "Superman" saga, it's simply the completion of yet another chapter.

For millions the world over, a whole *new* story of "Superman" is about to unfold.

This is just the beginning.

•　　•　　•

WHO'S WHO:
The Men And Women
Who Made "Superman."

The credits as they will appear on the screen . . .

CARD 1	ALEXANDER SALKIND PRESENTS
CARD 2	MARLON BRANDO
CARD 3	GENE HACKMAN
CARD 4	A RICHARD DONNER FILM
CARD 5	"SUPERMAN"
CARD 6	CHRISTOPHER REEVE
CARD 7	MARGOT KIDDER
CARD 8	NED BEATTY
CARD 9	JACKIE COOPER
CARD 10	GLENN FORD
CARD 11	TREVOR HOWARD
CARD 12	JACK O'HALLORAN
CARD 13	VALERIE PERRINE

CARD 14	MARIA SCHELL
CARD 15	TERENCE STAMP
CARD 16	PHYLLIS THAXTER
CARD 17	SUSANNAH YORK
CARD 18	JEFF EAST / MARC McCLURE
CARD 19	SARAH DOUGLAS / HARRY ANDREWS
CARD 20	PRODUCTION DESIGNER JOHN BARRY
CARD 21	PHOTOGRAPHED BY GEOFFREY UNSWORTH, B.S.C.
CARD 22	EDITOR STUART BAIRD
CARD 23	MUSIC BY JOHN WILLIAMS
CARD 24	SUPERMAN CREATED BY JERRY SIEGEL AND JOE SHUSTER
CARD 25	STORY BY MARIO PUZO
CARD 26	SCREENPLAY BY MARIO PUZO/DAVID NEWMAN LESLIE NEWMAN & ROBERT BENTON
CARD 27	CREATIVE CONSULTANT TOM MANKIEWICZ
CARD 28	ASSOCIATE PRODUCER CHARLES F. GREENLAW
CARD 29	EXECUTIVE PRODUCER ILYA SALKIND
CARD 30	PRODUCED BY PIERRE SPENGLER
CARD 31	DIRECTED BY RICHARD DONNER

AN ALEXANDER & ILYA
SALKIND PRODUCTION
A RICHARD DONNER FILM

CREATIVE SUPERVISOR & DIRECTOR OF SPECIAL EFFECTS	COLIN CHILVERS
CREATIVE SUPERVISOR OF OPTICAL VISUAL EFFECTS	ROY FIELD
ADDITIONAL SCRIPT MATERIAL BY	NORMAN ENFIELD
CREATIVE SUPERVISOR OF MATTES & COMPOSITES	LES BOWIE
MODEL EFFECTS DIRECTED & CREATED BY	DEREK MEDDINGS
ADDITIONAL MODEL EFFECTS	BRIAN SMITHIES
TITLES & SPECIAL VISUAL EFFECTS DESIGN	DENIS RICH
CREATIVE SUPERVISOR OF MAKE-UP & SPECIAL VISUALS	STUART FREEBORN
CASTING	LYNN STALMASTER
CONTINUITY SUPERVISOR	ELAINE SCHREYECK
CREATIVE DIRECTOR OF PROCESS PHOTOGRAPHY	DENYS COOP
ZOPTIC SPECIAL EFFECTS BY	ZORAN PERISIC
PRODUCTION EXECUTIVE	GEOFFREY HELMAN
2nd UNIT DIRECTION	DAVID TOMBLIN
	JOHN GLEN
	JOHN BARRY
	DAVID LANE
	PETER DUFFEL
	ROBERT LYNN
PROCESS UNIT DIRECTION	ANDRE DE TOTH
FILM EDITOR	MICHAEL ELLIS
SUPERVISING SOUND EDITOR	CHRIS GREENHAM
SUPERVISING EDITOR OF OPTICAL & SPECIAL EFFECTS	PETER WATSON
SOUND MIXED & RE-RECORDED BY	GORDON K. McCALLUM
PRODUCTION SUPERVISOR	ROBERT SIMMONDS
PRODUCTION SUPERVISOR FOR NORTH AMERICA	TIMOTHY BURRILL
PRODUCTION SUPERVISOR FOR NEW MEXICO	TIM HAMPTON

PRODUCTION MANAGER	DUSTY SYMONDS
EXECUTIVE ASSISTANT TO RICHARD DONNER	JEANNE FERBER
EXECUTIVE ASSISTANT TO THE PRODUCERS	MARIA MONREAL
PRODUCTION MANAGERS:	
NEW YORK	PETER RUNFOLO
ALBERTA	LES KIMBER
NEW MEXICO	AUSTEN JEWELL
LOCATION MANAGER— NEW YORK	CHRIS COLES
	DAVID LANE
VISUAL CO-ORDINATORS	ERNEST WALTER
	MICHAEL CAMPBELL
ASSISTANT DIRECTOR	DAVID TOMBLIN
CAMERA OPERATOR	PETER MacDONALD
SPECIAL EFFECTS CANADA & NEW YORK	JOHN RICHARDSON
SPECIAL EFFECTS NEW MEXICO	BOB MacDONALD
PRODUCTION CO-ORDINATOR	MICHAEL DUTHIE
ASSISTANT DIRECTOR & FLYING UNIT CO-ORDINATOR	DOMINIC FULFORD
ASSISTANT DIRECTORS	VINCENT WINTER
	MICHAEL DRYHURST
	ALLAN JAMES
	GARETH TANDY
U.S.A.	JERRY GRANDEY
	MICHAEL RAUCH
	BUD GRACE
2nd ASSISTANT DIRECTORS	STEVE LANNING
	ROY BUTTON
	MICHAEL GREEN
	KIERON PHIPPS
	CHARLES MARRIOTT
	VIC SMITH
	KEITH LUND
	MICHAEL HOOK
	PATRICK CADELL
	PETER JACOBS
	SIMON MILTON
	MICHAEL MURRAY
U.S.A.	PETER BERGQUIST
	CANDACE SUERSTEDT
TRAINEE ASSISTANTS	YVES GAUMONT
	PAUL STOREY

—213—

	WALDO ROEG
	BILL RUDGARD
CONTINUITY	KAY RAWLINGS
	DORIS MARTIN
U.S.A.	BETSY NORTON
ASSISTANT CONTINUITY	KATYA KOLPAKTCHY
ADDITIONAL CONTINUITY	JOSIE FULFORD
	RITA DAVISON
	ANGELA MARTELLI
PRODUCTIONS ASSISTANTS:	PAT CARR
	JEANNIE STONE
	ANN GREEN
	JEAN HALL
	LIZ GREEN
	JOY BAYLEY
	DIANE APPLEBY
	SALLY BALL
	NORMA HAZELDEN
	NORMA GARMENT
U.S.A.	ADELINE LEONARD
	DICK LIEBEGOTT
CANADA	PATTI ALLEN
SPECIAL UNIT	JENNIE McCLEAN
SECRETARIES	JANE COX
	JANE DIXIE
	SUE EDWARDS
SECRETARY TO THE	SUE HAUSNER
EXECUTIVE PRODUCER	
SECRETARY TO THE	TRUDY BALEN
PRODUCER	
ADDITIONAL	ALEX THOMSON
PHOTOGRAPHY	
MODEL PHOTOGRAPHY	PAUL WILSON
ADDITIONAL	JACK ATCHELER
PHOTOGRAPHY	
NEW MEXICO	ROBERT E. COLLINS
ALBERTA	REGINALD MORRIS
NEW YORK	SOL NEGRIN
ADDITIONAL MODEL	HARRY OAKES
PHOTOGRAPHY	BOB KINDRED
	LESLIE DEAR
U.S.A.	DARRYL ANDERSON
NEW YORK PROCESS	BOB BAILIN
PLATE PHOTOGRAPHY	
NEW YORK PROCESS	CERVIN ROBINSON
STILLS	
AERIAL PHOTOGRAPHY	PETER ALLWORK

CAMERA OPERATORS	JOHN HARRIS
	JIMMY DEVIS
	JOHN MORGAN
	MICHAEL FOX
	GORDON HAYMAN
	GEOFF GLOVER
	KEN COLES
	RONNIE FOX ROGERS
	GINGER GEMMELL
	ROY FORD
	JACK LOWEN
	GEORGE PINK
U.S.A.	LOU BARLIA
	JIM CONTNER
	MICHAEL CHEVALIER
	JACK COURTLAND
	HOWARD ANDERSON III
CANADA	ROD PARKHURST
MATTE CAMERA OPERATORS	PETER HARMAN
	PETER HAMMOND
WESSCAM PHOTOGRAPHY	RONALD GOODMAN
HELICOPTER PILOTS:	
NEW MEXICO	MARC WOLFF
NEW YORK	AL CERULLO
CAMERA ASSISTANTS	JOHN CAMPBELL
	JONATHAN TAYLOR
	TREVOR COOP
	PETER VERSEY
	RONNIE ANSCOMBE
	DAVID LENHAM
	JOHN DEATON
	ALAN GATWARD
U.S.A.	DOMENIC MASTRIPPOLITO
CANADA	TOM RYAN
MUSIC EDITOR	BOB HATHAWAY
ASSISTANT	KEN ROSS
FIRST ASSISTANT EDITOR	BOB MULLEN
ASSISTANT EDITORS	DAVID BEESLEY
	TIM JORDAN
	MIKE ROUND
	NEIL FARRELL
	CHRISTOPHER MORRIS
	COLIN WILSON
	GEORGE AKERS

SOUND EDITORS	
Effects	PETER PENNELL
Dialogues	MICHAEL HOPKINS
	PAT FOSTER
Footsteps & Effects	STAN FIFERMAN
	JOHN FOSTER
ASSISTANT DUBBING	GEOFF BROWN
EDITORS	LEONARD GREEN
	PATRICK BRENNAN
	JUPITER SEN
	TONY ORTON
	DAVID FISHER
ASSISTANT EDITOR OF	RUSSELL WOOLNOUGH
OPTICAL & SPECIAL	
EFFECTS	
SOUND MIXERS	ROY CHARMAN
	NORMAN BOLLAND
	BRIAN MARSHALL
U.S.A.	CHARLES SCHMITZ
	DICK RAGUSA
CANADA	CHRIS LARGE
ASSISTANTS	MICHAEL TUCKER
	GEORGE RICE
	KEITH PAMPLIN
	DES EDWARDS
SUPERVISING ART	MAURICE FOWLER
DIRECTOR, ENGLAND &	
NEW YORK	
SUPERVISING ART	BILL BRODIE
DIRECTOR, CANADA &	
NEW MEXICO	
ART DIRECTORS	NORMAN DORME
	NORMAN REYNOLDS
	ERNEST ARCHER
	TONY READING
	LES DILLEY
	STUART CRAIG
U.S.A.	GENE RUDOLF
	PHILIP BENNET
	STAN JOLLEY
DRAUGHTSMEN	TONY RIMMINGTON
	REG BREAM
	TED AMBROSE
	DENNIS BOSHER
	ALAN CASSIE
SET DECORATION	PETER HOWITT
U.S.A.	FRED WEILER

ILLUSTRATORS	IVOR BEDDOES
	ROY CARNON
	REG HILL
MODELLERS	JAN STEVENS
	PETER VOYSEY
SCENIC ARTISTS	ERNEST SMITH
	BILL BEAVIS
DECOR & LETTERING ARTIST	NORMAN HART
CONSTRUCTION MANAGERS	LARRY CLEARY
	JACK CARTER
U.S.A.	HARRY KERSEY
	HERMAN LOWERS
MODEL CONSTRUCTION MANAGER	MICHAEL REDDING
ASSISTANT CONSTRUCTION MANAGER	ROY EVANS
MODEL MAKERS	TERRY REED
	CYRIL FORSTER
	ANDREW KELLY
	JEFF LUFF
	TONY DUNSTERVILLE
	TADEUSZ KRZANOWSKI
SPECIAL EFFECTS TECHNICIANS	ROY SPENCER
	TERRY SCHUBERT
	BOB NUGENT
	JOE FITT
	RON BURTON
	BRIAN WARNER
	RODNEY FULLER
	MICHAEL DUNLEAVY
	JIMMY HARRIS
	PETER BIGGS
	FRANK RICHARDSON
	PETER PICKERING
PROPERTY MASTERS	GEORGE BALL
	DANNY SKUNDRIC
PROPS	EDDIE FRANCIS
PRODUCTION BUYERS	JOHN LANZER
	PETER PALMER
PRODUCTION ACCOUNTANT	DOUGLAS NOAKES
ASSISTANT ACCOUNTANT	GRAHAM HENDERSON
PUBLICIST	GORDON ARNELL
PUBLICITY ASSISTANTS	JUNE BROOM
	PAT O'REILLY
STILLS	BOB PENN
	DOUGLAS LUKE

—217—

COSTUMES DESIGNED BY	YVONNE BLAKE
WARDROBE SUPERVISOR &	BETTY ADAMSON
ADDITIONAL DESIGNS	
ADDITIONAL COSTUMES	RUTH MORLEY
WARDROBE ASSISTANTS	HELEN GILL
	EDDIE SILVA
	AUSTIN COOPER
	JANET TEBROOKE
	COLIN WILSON
	BARBARA GILLETT
	ELVIRA ANGELINETTA
MAKE-UP ARTISTS	PHILIP RHODES
	BASIL NEWALL
	KAY FREEBORN
	GRAHAM FREEBORN
	NICK MALEY
	SYLVIA CROFT
	CONNIE REEVE
U.S.A.	LOUIS LANE
CANADA	JAMIE BROWN
HAIRDRESSERS	PAT McDERMOTT
	JOAN WHITE
	STELLA RIVERS
	CATHY KEVANY
U.S.A.	DARBY HALPIN
CANADA	ILOE ELLIOTT
CHIEF ELECTRICIANS:	
Lee Electric	MAURICE GILLETT
Pinewood	JOHN TYTHE
ELECTRICIANS:	
Lee Electric	RAY EVANS
	RAY MEEHAN
Pinewood	JOHN MAY
	HARRY WOODLEY
	BERT BOSHER
	FRED WEBSTER
	JACK THETFORD
ENGLISH CASTING	MARY SELWAY
STUNT CO-ORDINATION	ALF JOINT
	VIC ARMSTRONG
NEW YORK	ALEX STEVENS
STUNT CO-ORDINATION	
ADDITIONAL STUNTS	PAUL WESTON
	GEORGE COOPER
	WENDY LEECH
	BILL WESTON
	STUART FELL

CANADA	DICK BUTLER
	RICHARD HACKMAN
ADDITIONAL MODEL EFFECTS	GEORGE GIBBS
FLYING SYSTEMS & PROCESS PROJECTION	WALLY VEEVERS
PROCESS SYSTEMS	CHARLES STAFFELL
TRAVELLING MATTE SUPERVISOR	DENNIS BARTLETT
OPTICAL LIAISON	MARTIN SHORTHALL (Harrow College of Technology & Art)
ZOPTIC OPERATION	DAVID SPEED
	MIKE DREW
	JAMES ASPINALL
MATTE ARTISTS	DOUG FERRIS
	RAY CAPLE
ASSISTANT MATTE ARTISTS	LIZ LETTMAN
FLYING EFFECTS	DEREK BOTELL
	BOB HARMAN
TITLE & SPECIAL OPTICAL SEQUENCES PHOTOGRAPHED BY	CAMERA EFFECTS LTD.
	ROY PACE
	SHELDON ELBOURNE
SPECIAL SEQUENCES	HOWARD A. ANDERSON CO.
	CONTINENTAL CAMERA SYSTEMS INC.
OPTICAL SEQUENCES	OXFORD SCIENTIFIC FILMS LTD.
	PETER PARKS
	SEAN MORRIS
	NATIONAL SCREENS SERVICES LTD.
	GILLIE POTTER PRODUCTIONS LTD.
	DELECLUSE REALISATIONS
	CINEMA RESEARCH CORPORATION
	VAN der VEER PHOTO EFFECTS
	RANK POST PRODUCTIONS LTD.
	CINEFEX (LONDON) LTD.
	VEE FILMS LTD.
	GENERAL SCREEN ENTERPRISES LTD.

VIDEO OPERATORS   CHRIS WARREN
                         BRIAN KING
MUSIC MIXED & RECORDED AT ANVIL STUDIOS BY
ERIC TOMLINSON.
MUSIC PLAYED BY THE LONDON SYMPHONY
ORCHESTRA.
ALL ORIGINAL COMPOSITIONS © 1978 WARNER
TAMERLANE PUBLISHING CORPORATION.
SOUND MIXED & RE-RECORDED AT PINEWOOD
STUDIOS.

In Memory of
TERRY HILL
JOHN BODIMEADE

CAST

JOR-EL	MARLON BRANDO
LEX LUTHOR	GENE HACKMAN
SUPERMAN/CLARK KENT	CHRISTOPHER REEVE
LOIS LANE	MARGOT KIDDER
OTIS	NED BEATTY
PERRY WHITE	JACKIE COOPER
PA KENT	GLENN FORD
1st ELDER	TREVOR HOWARD
NON	JACK O'HALLORAN
EVE TESCHMACHER	VALERIE PERRINE
VOND-AH	MARIA SCHELL
GENERAL ZOD	TERENCE STAMP
MA KENT	PHYLLIS THAXTER
LARA	SUSANNAH YORK
YOUNG CLARK KENT	JEFF EAST
JIMMY OLSEN	MARC McCLURE
URSA	SARAH DOUGLAS
2nd ELDER	HARRY ANDREWS

& IN ORDER OF APPEARANCE

KRYPTON COUNCIL

3rd ELDER	VASS ANDERSON
4th ELDER	JOHN HOLLIS
5th ELDER	JAMES GARBUTT
6th ELDER	MICHAEL GOVER
7th ELDER	DAVID NEAL
8th ELDER	WILLIAM RUSSELL
9th ELDER	PENELOPE LEE
10th ELDER	JOHN STUART
11th ELDER	ALAN CULLEN

BABY KAL-EL   LEE QUIGLEY
BABY CLARK KENT   AARON SMOLINSKI

SMALLVILLE

LANA LANG   DIANE SHERRY
COACH   JEFF ATCHESON
FOOTBALL PLAYER   BRAD FLOCK
TEAM MANAGER   DAVID PETROU

DAILY PLANET

1st EDITOR   BILLY J. MITCHELL
2nd EDITOR   ROBERT HENDERSON
1st REPORTER   LARRY LAMB
2nd REPORTER   JAMES BROCKINGTON
3rd REPORTER   JOHN CASSADY
4th REPORTER   JOHN F. PARKER
5th REPORTER   ANTONY SCOTT
6th REPORTER   RAY EVANS
7th REPORTER   SU SHIFRIN
8th REPORTER   MIQUEL BROWN
1st COPY BOY   VINCENT MARZELLO
2nd COPY BOY   BENJAMIN FEITELSON
1st SECRETARY   LISE HILBOLDT
2nd SECRETARY   LEUEEN WILLOUGHBY
PERRY'S SECRETARY   JILL INGHAM
WINDOW CLEANER   PIETER STUYCK

METROPOLIS

REX REED   REX REED
MUGGER   WESTON GAVIN
OFFICER 1   STEPHEN KAHAN
OFFICER 2   RAY HASSETT
OFFICER 3   RANDY JURGENSON
NEWS VENDOR   MATT RUSSO

SUPERMAN'S 1st NIGHT

PILOT   COLIN SKEAPING
PIMP   BO RUCKER
TV CAMERAMAN   PAUL AVERY
BURGLAR   DAVID BAXT
PATROLMAN MOONEY   GEORGE HARRIS II
1st HOOD   MICHAEL HARRIGAN
2nd HOOD   JOHN CORDING
3rd HOOD   RAYMOND THOMPSON
4th HOOD   OZ CLARKE

DESK SERGEANT	REX EVERHARDT
LITTLE GIRL	JAYNE TOTTMAN
AIR FORCE ONE PILOT	FRANK LAZARUS
CO PILOT	BRIAN PROTHEROE
1st CREWMAN	LAWRENCE TRIMBLE
2nd CREWMAN	ROBERT WHELAN
3rd CREWMAN	DAVID CALDER
NEWSCASTER	NORWICK DUFF
NEWSCASTER	KEITH ALEXANDER
NEWSCASTER	MICHAEL ENSIGN

CONCORDE

PILOT	MICHAEL BEHR
PILOT	JOHN REES

MISSILE CONVOYS

MAJOR	LARRY HAGMAN
SGT. HAYLEY	PAUL TUERPE
LIEUTENANT	GRAHAM McPHERSON
PETTY OFFICER	DAVID YORSTON

MISSILE CONTROL

ADMIRAL	ROBERT O'NEILL
GENERAL	ROBERT MacLEOD
1st CONTROLLER	JOHN RATZENBERGER
STATE SENATOR	PHIL BROWN
2nd SENATOR	BILL BAILEY

PENTAGON

JOINT CHIEF OF GENERAL STAFF	BRUCE BOA

GOLF COURSE

AGENT	BURNELL TUCKER

CALIFORNIA

INDIAN CHIEF	CHIEF TUG SMITH
SUPERCHIEF DRIVER	NORMAN WARWICK
ASSISTANT	CHUCK JULIAN
POWER CO. DRIVER	COLIN ETHERINGTON
MATE	MARK WYNTER

PRISON

WARDEN	ROY STEVENS

CARD A

The story, all names, characters and incidents portrayed in this production are fictitious. No indentification with actual persons, places and buildings is intended or should be inferred.

This motion picture is protected by the copyright laws of the United States of America and other countries throughout the world. Any unauthorised exhibition, distribution or copying of this film or any part thereof (including soundtrack) is an infringement of the copyright and will subject the infringer to severe civil and criminal penalties.

CARD B

FILMED IN PANAVISION®
PROCESSED BY TECHNICOLOR®

CARD C

(LOGO) FOR DOLBY STEREO DOLBY SOUND CONSULTANT	MAX BELL
AERIAL CAMERA SEQUENCES	WESSCAM
CHEMTONE SEQUENCES BY	TVC LABORATORY INC.

CARD D

CAMERA EQUIPMENT SUPPLIED BY	SAMUELSON FILM SERVICE LTD.
LIGHTING EQUIPMENT BY	LEE ELECTRIC (LIGHTING) LTD.
COSTUMES BY	BERMANS & NATHANS LTD.

CARD E

CLARK KENT'S WARDROBE FURNISHED BY	BARNEYS INC.
JEWELRY BY	CARTIER
TV & AUDIO BY	J.V.C.
CHEERIOS BY	GENERAL MILLS INC.
WATCHES BY	TIMEX

CARD F

THE PRODUCERS WISH TO THANK:
THE MAYOR'S OFFICE FOR MOTION PICTURES & TELEVISION, NEW YORK.

THE NEW MEXICO STATE FILM COMMISSION.
THE ALBERTA GOVERNMENT FILM INDUSTRY
DEVELOPMENT BOARD.
CANADIAN PACIFIC RAILWAYS.
THE NATIONAL SATELLITE VISUAL SURVEY SPACE
COUNCIL FOR SPACE PHOTOGRAPHY.

CARD G

BASED UPON THE CHARACTER *SUPERMAN* APPEARING
IN COMICS AND MAGAZINES PUBLISHED BY
DC COMICS INC.

CARD H

COPYRIGHT © FILM EXPORT A.G. MCMLXXVIII
ALL TRADE MARKS OWNED BY & ALL CHARACTERS
© 1978 DC COMICS INC.
ALL RIGHTS RESERVED.
(LOGO) MPAA APPROVED NO. 25403
SALES CONSULTANT—ARMAND RUBIN

CARD I

MADE BY DOVEMEAD LIMITED
AT PINEWOOD STUDIOS, IVER HEATH, BUCKS,
ENGLAND.

AND ON LOCATION IN CANADA & THE UNITED STATES
OF AMERICA AND AT SHEPPERTON STUDIO CENTRE,
ENGLAND.

CARD J

AN INTERNATIONAL FILM PRODUCTION INC. PICTURE

CARD K

AN ALEXANDER SALKIND PRESENTATION

CARD L

DISTRIBUTED BY WARNER BROS.